4,000 questions *for* getting to know anyone *and* everyone

BARBARA ANN KIPFER

Random House Reference
New York · Toronto · London · Sydney · Auckland

4,000 Questions for Getting to Know Anyone and Everyone

Copyright © 2004 by Barbara Ann Kipfer

This book is available for special discounts for bulk purchases for sales promotions or premiums. Special editions, including personalized covers, excerpts of existing books, and corporate imprints, can be created in large quantities for special needs. For more information, write to Special Markets/ Premium Sales, 1745 Broadway, MD 6-2, New York, NY, 10019 or e-mail specialmarkets@randomhouse.com.

Visit the Random House Reference Web site:
www.randomwords.com

Typeset and printed in the United States of America.

Library of Congress cataloging-in-publication data is available.

ISBN: 0-375-72081-2

First Edition
0 9 8 7 6 5

DEDICATION

*There is never a quiet day
in our house!
Thank you to my dear husband,
Paul Magoulas, and to my
favorite talking heads,
Kyle and Keir.
Keep those questions coming!*

CONTENTS

5

INTRODUCTION

In the age of television and the computer, have we forgotten how to talk and really get to know each other? We interact all the time electronically . . . but how well?

4,000 Questions for Getting to Know Anyone and Everyone is a book filled with questions for conversation starters, small talk, interviews, and major discussions. I wrote this book because it was fun for me. Imagine my surprise when my teenaged son and his girlfriend each asked for a copy of the manuscript. They used it on the telephone and with it they honed their communication skills and laughed a lot.

Use this book to reclaim the lost art of conversation. *4,000 Questions for Getting to Know Anyone and Everyone* is also for conversations at the supper table, for an alternative to watching TV or playing video games, for dinners out with your companion, for party entertainment, for discussions with classmates or coworkers, for getting to know someone you are dating, and for making friends and developing deeper friendships. I suggest you write you own questions in the book and personalize it!

Childhood
& School

Where did you grow up?

Where did you go to school?

Did you have a special place where you went to be alone as a child?

How did you rebel as a child?

What did you hide from your parents?

Are you the same person you were as a child, or much different?

Talk about a time when you got into trouble at school.

Do you consider your childhood a happy one?

What is your saddest memory?

What were your first words and who told you what they were?

Do you have any siblings?

Was there anything unusual about your birth?

Who did you think was the smartest person in the world?

What was your most memorable toy?

Who had the most positive influence on you?

Why were you given your name and does it have a special meaning?

Did you have your own telephone growing up, or any other special privileges?

Did you ever get lost?

What is a special compliment you always received?

In what organizations and extracurricular activities did you participate?

What was the craziest thing you did in your youth?

What secret fantasies and games did you have as a child that you told no one about?

What activities besides eating went on at the kitchen table in the home you grew up in?

What has changed most about the neighborhood you grew up in?

Did you ever run away from home?

What about being a child do you miss the most?

What do you wish you had started to learn as a kid?

What tokens of your childhood do you wish you had saved?

Did you enjoy physical education in school?

What were your hobbies?

What childhood address(es) and phone number(s) do you remember?

How did you get to school?

What scary creatures did you think were in your childhood bedroom?

What was the most fun subject in elementary school, and what was the subject you dreaded the most?

At what age did you start school?

Where did you grow up?

Did you try to grow up in a hurry?

What is something you often did on Sundays?

Where did your family go on vacation?

Would you consider yourself well-behaved or badly-behaved?

If you had siblings, did you get along with them?

What significant historic events took place during your elementary school days?

What did you look forward to the most as a child?

CAN YOU DESCRIBE YOUR FIRST . . .

. . . memory?

. . . time left alone at home?

. . . day at school?

. . . punishment for doing something bad?

. . . childhood crush?

. . . experience with death?

. . . great accomplishment?

What did you wish for more often and/
or more sincerely than anything else?

What do you remember of the lessons
you were taught in elementary school?

What is one of your best and worst
childhood memories?

What did you fear most about
becoming an adult?

What was the remedy for the common
cold in your home?

What was the most difficult thing to
overcome from your childhood?

What details do you remember
of your childhood bedroom(s)?

What playground activities did you
like best?

Are there foods, smells, flavors,
sounds, songs, etc. that bring back
memories of your childhood?

What was the first book you
remember reading just for fun?

What did your childhood bedroom
look like?

Do you think that learning
takes place in the womb?

What is your most vivid
memory of elementary school?

What is something you really wish
you had not started earlier in life?

Did you do as you were told
when young or did you rebel?

What big events happened in the year you were born and who was president?

Children's stories: how you think they have changed?

Was there anything unusual that happened to you in childhood?

Would your parents consider you well-behaved or badly-behaved?

Who was one of your most memorable teachers in elementary school?

What early lesson from childhood have you continued to follow throughout life?

Did you have any serious accidents as a child?

DO YOU REMEMBER . . .

. . . your bedtime rituals?

. . . what you dreamed of being when you grew up?

. . . your idols?

. . . a gift you made for someone?

. . . an incident in a school lunch room?

. . . your chores?

. . . who told you about the birds and bees?

. . . what you daydreamt about?

. . . any childhood illnesses?

. . . your first big disappointment?

. . . your most embarrassing moment?

What is one modern-day convenience you did not have as a child that was easy to live without?

What grade in elementary school did you enjoy most?

What were you called when you were younger and how did you feel about it?

What book had the biggest influence on you?

Were you spanked?

What would you change about your childhood and why?

Who, if anyone, was at home when you returned from school?

What kind of place was the city or town you grew up in?

What mementos of your early childhood do you have?

When you got caught for doing something wrong as a child, did you blame someone else, deny you did it, run and hide, or take responsibility?

What from your childhood proved most valuable?

When you were young, were you allowed to complain when the going got rough?

What fads did you embrace while growing up?

What were you most afraid of?

Did you ever play hooky?

As a kid, I missed a chance to _____.

What childhood or high school dreams are you now glad never came true?

What especially attracted and fascinated you as a child?

If you could choose your childhood and youth to live over again, how would it be different?

Name five childhood accomplishments.

Did you have any pets?

How did you find out that boys and girls are different?

What advice do you wish you had taken from your parents?

What was a frightening event from your childhood?

In one word describe yourself as a child.

What was the hardest thing about growing up?

What did you wear when younger that mortifies you now?

What serious illnesses or accidents did you have as a child?

What stories have you been told about yourself as a baby?

WHAT WERE YOUR FAVORITE . . .

... books?

... foods?

... games?

... mentors/role models?

... hiding places?

... classes?

... summer vacations?

... words?

... TV shows?

... bedtime stories or lullabies?

... campfire stories?

... dreams?

... memories?

... baby-sitters?

... pets?

... photos?

... collections or lucky charms?

... nursery rhymes?

What buzzword or phrase was highly popular during your teenage years?

Did you have teenage skin problems?

How was your birthday usually celebrated?

What was a fad in the decade in which you were born?

As a child, how did people describe you?

What is one thing every kid should have?

Did you go to camp?

Did religion play a part in your childhood social activities?

What is one thing you really
disliked as a child that you now
fully appreciate?

Did you believe in the tooth fairy?

What is the most mischievous
thing you recall doing?

Were you generally popular or
unpopular? Why?

As a kid, I lacked _____.

What qualities do you feel
make you different as an adult
from your childhood?

What object do you remember
vividly from your childhood?

Do you think schools should include
home economics in early education?

Was your childhood carefree
or full of worries?

What did you do when you
came home from school?

What did you teach yourself?

Did you prefer English or
science class?

Where did your high school
crowd hang out?

In class or lecture room, did you sit in
front or in an inconspicuous place?

What are the biggest gaps in
your education?

Did you study more than party
or party more than study?

Which teacher would be most
proud of you and which one would be
the most disappointed in you?

What is one thing that should
be different in schools ten years
from now?

What are your strongest memories
of elementary school, junior high,
and high school?

What were your high school colors,
mascot, cheers, and school song?

Of what early accomplishment
are you the most proud?

Are state and local officials working
toward better public education?

What is the way you like best
to learn?

Has anyone from your hometown
become famous?

Was there ever a bully in your life?
What was he or she like?

Is it possible to agree on a basic
set of values to teach schoolchildren?
Which ones?

Did you cram all night before exams?

What subject do you know
better than any other?

What grade would you like to
substitute teach for two months?

Have you ever cheated on a test
or paper?

What school books do you remember?

What was the number of students in
your high school graduating class?

What things do you
remember about your childhood
neighborhood(s)?

What was the name of your
high school?

Do you remember your high school
locker combination?

Do you think your school gave
you a quality education?

Did you learn to remember
through association?

What do you do now to
continue your education?

What was the most foolish thing
you did in high school?

What made the best teacher you
have ever had the best?

What school would you like to
have attended?

If you could learn anything at all,
what would it be?

Are you in favor of public
schools teaching morals and
moral behavior?

What did you do in study hall?

Did you learn how to speed-read
or speed-write?

What did you discover about yourself
in high school?

What subjects in school were
completely useless to you?

What subject would you study if you
had a year to devote to it?

If you were a teacher, what subject
would you like to teach?

Did you like decorating when
you were a child?

What was your favorite place
to do homework and what were
your homework rituals?

What is something you know more
about than anyone you know?

Did you ever go to the
principal's office?

What is something in the past
week that reminded you of your
childhood?

What is something you wish
you could have learned with the
snap of your fingers?

What were your extracurricular
activities in junior high and high
school?

What students did you admire
most in high school?

What is one thing you never did in high school that you wish you would have you done?

What new course would you like to add to the nation's school curriculum?

What do you think of private versus public school education?

Did you go to college?

Why did you go or not go to college?

What colleges did you apply to, if any?

How and where did you hang out in college?

What was your major in college and how did you pick it?

IF YOU COULD CHOOSE, WOULD YOU . . .

. . . *live your childhood over again?*

. . . *have grown up in a different decade or era?*

. . . *have been a more competitive kid?*

. . . *have learned more in the "classroom of life" than in school?*

. . . *have been a leader or a follower?*

. . . *take back something you did? If so, what?*

. . . *have been nicer to your parents?*

. . . *have changed your appearance?*

. . . *have worked harder in school?*

. . . *have made more friends?*

. . . *have had more belongings?*

What childlike quality have you maintained throughout your life?

Do you have fonder memories of high school or college?

What could you not have made it through high school or college without?

Did you graduate from college in debt or debt-free?

What did you look like as a teenager?

What was a very difficult educational experience for you?

What is one of the most important things about life you learned in school?

Why did you pick the college you did?

Did you get rejected by any colleges? If so, which ones?

What was the toughest course you have ever taken and how did you get through it?

Who are some famous graduates of your college?

What was a seminar or workshop that really stuck with you?

What is a subject you think should be offered in school?

What is an area in which you would be able to teach to others?

What kind of grades did you get throughout school?

What were the fads during your teen years?

What one subject you wish you had studied in school?

What word would you not want to spell in a spelling bee?

Were you a serious student or did you play too much?

Talk about grades and report cards.

Is the aim of schooling to teach how to think or to teach certain skills and facts?

Do you prepare thoroughly for tests?

What is the most important skill to have in school?

The most difficult thing in life is learning _____.

Should music be part of a well-rounded education?

What historical document (or part of one) do you think every American should know by heart?

What was the funniest thing someone wrote in your yearbook?

Would you consider getting a distance-learning degree?

Were there any college professors who really influenced you and how?

Where did you live when attending college?

DID YOU EVER . . .

. . . attend a high school or college reunion?

. . . learn a text or portion of text by heart?

. . . turn in a cheater on a test or paper?

. . . earn an award at school?

. . . go to a prom?

. . . skip school?

. . . get suspended?

. . . learn Esperanto?

. . . take an IQ test?

. . . have a curfew?

. . . join a fraternity or sorority?

What brands were extremely trendy during your teenage years?

Which foreign language would you most like to learn and why?

What big college events do you recall?

What foreign language should students be required to learn?

How did you pick your college and what it was known for?

Have you ever gone back to visit your old school?

If cost was not a factor, would you go to private school?

If you had to do it all over again, would you work harder in school to learn more?

What foreign languages do you speak?

Do you still use any foreign languages you spoke while growing up?

What is one course you would like to retake?

What lessons have you learned between youth and now?

What were the largest and smallest schools you attended?

How do you learn best: by listening, watching, reading, or doing?

Would you rather have school paid for but not get a choice of where to go or go anywhere but have to pay for your education?

Did you receive financial aid for school?

What are things you once believed that more knowledge proved different?

How has your hometown changed since you were a kid?

What magical things happened in your childhood that you still cannot explain?

What was the one thing you worried about most?

What year in school would you like to do over?

Do you raise your hand and ask questions?

How has your high school changed since you went there?

Did you make the most of your high school years?

What is still the same about you as when you were young?

What mentors, dead or alive, do you wish you had access to?

What about you as a child do you hope people will remember?

How did growing up change you?

When looking back at your childhood, what do you and do you not want to repeat?

Family
& Friends

If you only had one quarter,
who would you call?

As a child, were you closer to your
mother or father?

What troubles did you have
with your parents?

Which parent are you closest to now?

Do you have any siblings?

Are you close to your siblings?

Do you know what your mother's
or father's childhood was like?

What is your ancestry and ethnic
background?

How many generations can you
trace of your family's heritage?

What ancestor of yours would
you like to meet the most?

What is your most painful memory of
your father?

What is your most painful memory
of your mother?

What is an embarrassing thing
you found out about your parents?

What is your mother's cologne?

What is your father's aftershave?

Who is the best cook in your family?

What was your parents'
relationship like?

What might you have been like
if you had had perfect nurturing?

What did you learn from
your parents?

What things did your parents
argue about when you were little?

Who is the most serious person in
your family?

What family member do you
take after the most?

Has anyone in your family
been divorced?

What genetic diseases run
in your family?

How was your relationship with your
family when you first left home?

Who is the funniest person
in your family?

Are your parents married or divorced?

Talk about a family secret or
skeleton in the family closet.

What members of your family would
you like to write or call that you
have not kept in touch with?

What do you contribute
to your family?

What would your reaction be if
a close family member announced
he or she was gay?

What are the most important
things you learned from your father?

Would you like to have more brothers and sisters?

What is your happiest memory of your mother?

What stories were told about your grandparents?

Have you been to your ancestors' homeland?

What family tradition would you love to continue and pass on?

What is an attribute of your own mother you see most in yourself?

Do you look up to or avoid a brother or sister?

If you did not know your parents, what two people would you choose as your mother and father?

What things are you good at that your parents were good at too?

Your mother often said _____.

How did your parents feel about their own parents?

How do you feel about your family?

Who were your father's heroes?

What were the special stories
your grandparents told you?

What is the single most important
piece of advice you would offer to
newlyweds?

Are you interested in your genealogical
background?

What is an attribute of your own
father you see most in yourself?

What does your ethnic and cultural
background mean to you?

What is something memorable
that you experienced that your
children will probably never get to
experience?

What do you wish your parents
would have told you while you were
still a kid?

What would you do if your sibling
told you that he or she killed someone
in a hit-and-run accident? Would you
turn him or her in?

What is your most beautiful childhood
memory of your parents?

Your father often said _____.

What things did you love doing with
your family?

What family heirlooms do you
have and how did you get them?

If you could give an award to someone in your family, what would it be?

What are all the things you would like or you would have liked to say to your mother?

What was something your parents did for fun?

What are/were your parents' names and what did you call them?

Who is the "talker" of your family and who is the "listener"?

What troubles did you have with your mom when growing up?

What is one thing you would change about your parents?

What funny or crazy experience do you remember from a family gathering or vacation?

For what reasons are you proud of your sibling(s)?

What was your favorite stuffed animal?

Have you or your family been affected by a natural disaster?

What patterns have been handed down over generations?

What is the last place you went to for a family vacation?

What are your opinions about divorce?

When was a time your family was in danger?

What is the biggest mystery
in your family?

Could you sketch your family tree?

What do you think about young
adults living with parents?

Did you play with your cousins?

Did your family experience a
tragedy during your childhood?

Does your brother or sister
embarrass or enchant you?

Were your grandparents born in
America? If not, how did they get
to America?

What do you think is the worst part
of having a close family?

Do you wish you were born into
a big family, medium-sized family,
or as an only child?

If you had the power, how would you
change your family?

What would a typical evening be
like when your parents entertained
friends?

What is the thing you disagree about
most as a family?

What was a family project you
worked on as a child?

What family trait would you like
to pass on to your descendants?

How do you feel about having
relatives stay with you?

IF YOU HAD TO CHOOSE, WOULD YOU . . .

. . . hang out with your dad or your mom on a Saturday night?

. . . have left home at age fifteen or still live there now?

. . . dress like your parents or act like them?

. . . lie to your mom or to your significant other?

. . . be the oldest child or the baby of the family?

. . . be an only child or one of ten children?

What was the birth order among your siblings?

What was something you and a brother or sister did together regularly?

How would you describe your father or mother?

Describe something you and your father or mother did together.

What is something that made your mother or father happy?

Can you make some predictions for your children, grandchildren?

What was something you like(d) about one of your relatives?

How strong are your relationships with the members of your original family?

With what family member would you most like to work?

What character or physical traits did you inherit from your mother and father?

Who were your mother's idols?

Do you know your family's
special recipes?

How often did your parents say they
loved you when you were young?

How did your mother and father meet?

If your ancestors emigrated
from another country, from where
did they come?

Describe the "ideal" family.

What is one of the ways you
and a brother or sister are alike?

What arguments did you have
over and over with your parents?

What are the ways you tried
to make your parents happy?

How warm is your family?

What is your most horrifying
childhood memory of your parents?

Who in your family do you most
look like?

How did your grandparents get here?

Where did they settle and why?

What hobbies did your parents
have during your childhood?

What do you depend on
your family for?

What values did your parents
instill in you?

What do you think of families with two mothers or two fathers?

How did you typically get into trouble with your parents and how were you punished?

What is your father's work?

Would you care for your parents in their old age?

What unanswered question would you like to ask your grandparents?

What is something you did as a child that your parents still do not know about?

Who had more influence on you: mother or father?

Where was the secret hideout of your youth?

When you were young, were you told you could do or be anything you wanted?

What would make you feel betrayed by your mate?

What do you think about mandatory premarital counseling?

Do you think that kids raised in households without fathers are at a disadvantage?

In your family, did everyone have their own seat at the dinner table?

What do you remember about your oldest relative(s) whom you knew personally?

What people did you have to
take care of while growing up?

Did you play tricks on your siblings?

Are you the same person with your
family as with your friends; if not,
what are the differences and why?

Tell a story of an eccentric relative.

What is your happiest memory
of your father?

What do you like about
your sibling(s)?

What are your sisters and brothers
like and what do they do?

Were your parents happy with
the circumstances of their lives?

Can you recall a specific incident
that got you into trouble at home?

What was the most memorable
family outing?

WHAT IF . . .

. . . you were infertile; would you adopt?

*. . . a friend of yours wanted a shotgun/whirlwind wedding;
would you advise against it?*

. . . you found out you were adopted; how would you feel?

. . . you discovered one of your parents having an affair?

. . . you were a child again; what would you tell your parents?

*. . . you could change how you handled your most significant
relationship; what would you do differently?*

Do you think you said or have said
"I love you" enough to your mother
and father?

What did your grandparents
do for a living?

Do you feel that your parents did
a bad, fair, good, or excellent job in
raising you?

What was your upbringing: rich,
poor, or middle class?

How often would you like to
see your parents?

What is the first thing that comes to
mind when you think of your family?

What lessons did your parents feel
strongly about passing on to you?

How did you usually eat dinner
as a family growing up?

What deaths in the family affected
you strongly?

Recall the first time you saw
your siblings.

What family vacations were taken
and where? What was a particularly
memorable one?

Which relative did you or
do you get along best with?

What do you think your
parents worried about when
they were your age?

Did you ever feel ashamed of
either of your parents?

Describe your grandmothers.

Did your parents split up or divorce?

Name something you like or admire about someone in your family.

Would (or do) your parents make good grandparents?

What is one thing you would like to have changed in your mother's life?

What is the nicest thing a brother or sister ever did for you?

What is the oldest family photograph that you have?

What is the location of your family's memorabilia?

What was one of your mother's strongest characteristics?

What is one of the ways your mother and grandmother were/are alike (or father and grandfather)?

What would you really like to say to your brother or sister?

Does your family have strong traditions that you still observe?

How much time did your parents spend with you when you were a child?

Did your parents choose a legal guardian for you if they died prematurely? If so, who?

What advice do you offer for getting along with stepparents?

Can you love your stepparents
or adopted parents as much as
a biological parent?

Who is the most musical member
of your family?

What is one thing you would like to
have changed in your father's life?

In my house, we never had enough
_____.

What things about your parents
worry you?

What decision would you like
your family to make regarding your
life if you were mentally or physically
incapacitated?

Are you better off than
your parents were?

Did/do your parents understand you?

Do you think intelligence
is related to genetics?

How did your parents react
to your grades?

What person in your family would you
like to travel back in time to meet?

What do you know about your
parents' values, philosophies, and
religious beliefs?

What was one of the more
unique aspects of your family
when growing up?

What is something you wish
for your father?

What was the worst trouble
you were in with your parents?

Who are two famous people
you would have liked as parents?

What person from your family
do you most admire?

Which is better: being a parent
or grandparent?

How did you get along with your
parents, especially as a teenager?

How much do you care about
your genealogy?

With what family member have
you regrettably lost touch?

What will be the one thing you will
miss about your parents when they
are no longer alive?

What member of your family do you
feel closest to and why?

WHO IS . . .

. . . *your most eccentric relative?*

. . . *your most famous ancestor?*

. . . *your family ashamed of?*

. . . *your family particularly proud of?*

. . . *your namesake?*

. . . *your favorite relative apart from your parents and siblings?*

. . . *the family member most similar to you?*

. . . *a family member that you have distanced yourself from?*

. . . *the relative you most enjoy visiting?*

Who has the largest family you know?

What was an issue that caused
a great rift between your parents
and yourself?

Describe a typical family dinner.

Who in the family do you have the
most difficulty communicating with?

What family reunions have
you attended?

Describe your grandfathers.

How much affection did your
parents show for each other?

What family events or activities
give you happy memories?

What objects do you remember
from your parents' living room?

What could your family plan
that would make you happy?

What is one thing you really
appreciate about your family?

What are the most important things
you learned from your mother?

Describe something of significance that
someone in your family has taught you.

What do you and your siblings
have in common?

Have you accomplished more than
your parents?

What things were important
to you as a teenager?

What did you do during the
summers as a kid?

What do you know about your
mother's work and responsibilities?

Did you ever have to care for
or parent one of your parents when
you were a child?

What are the stupidest rules
your parents had?

What warnings and old wives'
tales were you taught growing up?

What activity or event do you
think every family should experience
together at least once?

Has your mother and father said
"I love you" enough?

What was one of your father's
strongest characteristics?

What is a trait you do not share
with your siblings?

Which aunt(s) and uncle(s) were
important to you?

What (if anything) do you
remember or know about your
great-grandparents?

What is a very happy memory you
have of your family?

Describe your last family reunion
and how many relatives attended?

Did you become who you are because
of or in spite of your parents?

What is the way your sibling(s) and you act toward each other now?

Do little sisters and brothers have it easier or harder than older siblings?

What word or phrase describes your mother's or father's personality?

Describe your parents' marriage while you were growing up.

What game(s) or song(s) did your family play or sing while traveling in the car?

Have either of your parents ever said they were sorry or asked your forgiveness?

What is a concern you have for a family member?

Did anyone in your family know someone or have an encounter with someone really famous?

How do you remember playing with siblings?

In what way are you and a parent alike?

How would you change the rules your parents gave you?

In what ways (if any) have alcohol or drugs affected your family?

Who wins most of your family arguments?

What kind of work did your mother's parents do?

What kind of work did your father's parents do?

Are either of your parents deceased?
If so, who?

What do you dislike the most
in the person in your family with
whom you most resemble?

What present did you get from your
parents that sticks in your memory?

What are three things you like
and dislike about your parents?

Is interracial marriage okay
or not okay?

Who is the most patient/
helpful/generous/loving member
of the family?

What were your parents' most
distinguishing features?

What is the way your sibling(s) and
you acted toward each other as kids?

What family member would every
adult do well to emulate?

How would your father or mother
describe his or her father or mother?

What are your family's traits:
hotheads, worriers, avoiders
of conflict?

What would you like to do
for your parents to make their life
more enjoyable?

Who lived the longest in
your family's history?

WHAT IS YOUR
FAMILY'S MOST MEMORABLE . . .

. . . tradition?

. . . holiday decoration?

. . . vacation?

. . . saying?

. . . feud?

. . . heirloom?

What is the most surprising thing you learned about your parents' childhood?

Was there a time when your parents really embarrassed you?

What is the silliest thing your parents ever did?

What do/did you like about your parents?

Describe each family member in one word.

Why do moms and dads fight?

Tell a story you heard about one of your aunts or uncles.

Are you friends with your cousins?

How often do you contact your siblings?

Would you invite one of your parents to live with you if he or she was all alone and older?

Was yours a religious family
or one that went to church in
an obligated way?

Which of your male or female
relatives served in the armed forces?

What is an endearing characteristic
of your family?

Describe your mother's most
annoying habit.

What three instructions would you
leave loved ones on getting through
life successfully?

People should not have children
before what age?

How did your parents handle
the empty-nest experience?

Tell a story you heard about
one of your ancestors.

Have you ever caught your
parents having sex?

Does marriage mean the same
to you as to your parents?

Would you want your marriage
to be like that of your parents?

What was your relationship with your
parents when you were a teenager?

What were your most
memorable experiences shared
with your grandparents?

What sights, smells, or sounds do you
remember from your grandparents'
houses?

What is something your parents did that you have never forgiven them for and what would it take for you to forgive them?

What is something you wish for your mother?

Are your parents proud of what you have accomplished?

What things did you see or overhear that no one knew about?

What are your grandparents' names and where did/do they live?

What did/do you call your grandparents?

What advice did your parents give you that you remember and use?

What is one thing you are especially glad your parents told you?

Tell a memory of your grandmother or grandfather.

How was affection expressed in your family growing up?

What are your parents like?

Describe your family's economic conditions and how that affected your lifestyle.

Who usually calls more often: your parents or you?

What excuses do you use to not see relatives?

Would you ever let a relative live with you? Why or why not?

Who were your parents' friends while you were growing up?

Have you been able to forgive your mother and father for their failures and imperfections?

When did you ever feel sorry for your parents?

What things do you hide when your family comes to visit?

What does true friendship mean?

When you meet people for the first time, what are you most interested in learning about them?

What was your most embarrassing moment in front of a group?

Are you a leader?

Who brings out the best in you?

Does being around people drain or motivate you?

Can you recognize friends by their scent?

How have friends enriched your life?

What is your favorite person to gossip with?

What do your friends find likable about you?

Would you rather be caught naked by a friend or stranger?

What friend taught you an important lesson about life?

HAVE YOU EVER . . .

. . . stopped speaking with your parents for a long period of time?

. . . blamed your parents for your own flaws?

. . . told a friend or family member what you honestly think of him or her?

. . . forgiven someone who hurt you?

. . . had a friend who became like a member of your family?

. . . had to make a great sacrifice for a relative?

When I am in a large group, I _____.

What family or person you know seems genuinely happy?

Who once came to your "rescue" and how?

Who is your best friend?

Would you rather spend time with your family or with your friends?

With whom would you like to develop a closer relationship?

You are embarrassed when you _____.

How do you like to show love to people who are special to you?

What friend do you miss the most?

What friends did you stick by when they went through a tough time?

What friend is most like you?

Would you betray a friend to get something you really want?

Is there someone you confide in
or do you keep troubles to yourself?

Whose life have you made better
(other than a family member)?

What people of great potential
have you known and what happened
to them?

How sociable are you?

Would you rather die without
warning or die slowly surrounded by
family and friends?

What friends do you feel most and
least comfortable with and why?

Describe your best friends during
your teen years.

Whose party above all others
will you never forget?

For years, I have missed and
wondered about _____.

Is there anybody you just do not
get along with?

What contributions do you dream
of making to others?

Who is the most loving person
you know?

Who is someone who listens when
you talk to him or her?

What people are you not talking
to anymore?

Who has really changed your life?

If you gave a party for all your friends, would they already know each other?

Who are the friends that went with you from elementary school through high school?

What is your limit for touching between platonic friends?

Whose advice do you listen to?

What is your favorite family photo?

Who is the most innocent person you know?

What friend do you not take seriously?

From whom have you received unconditional love and acceptance?

What room(s) do you like to gather in with friends?

Would you rather confront someone about lying or let it slide and try to forget about it?

What birthday party with friends do you remember well?

What clubs, social groups, and organizations do you belong to now?

In your closest relationships, what is the connection between intimacy and independence?

Would you rather have three very good friends or unlimited acquaintances?

What social situations make you flustered or nervous?

What was your family's favorite
snack when you were growing up?

What social or country club
would you like to belong to?

Who do you usually spend
the holidays with?

How important is it for you
to be popular?

When people first meet you, you are
afraid they will think _____ about you.

Do you deliberately make friends
with people you think can help you?

What friend is most unlike you?

Do you stick by a friend even
if they hurt you?

How often have you kept in touch
with people you promised you would?

Do you get so angry that you shout at
people who are closest to you?

Name ten people you know and like.

Do you prefer company or solitude?

How do you most often
communicate your feelings to close
friends when they are not near?

What clubs, social groups,
and organizations did you used to
belong to and why do you not
belong anymore?

What is one topic you believe
you should avoid discussing
with those closest to you?

Do your friends tend to have
easygoing or difficult personalities?

If you could spend a vacation with
one person, who would it be?

What people do you wish you
had not trusted?

Have you ever given someone a
nickname you knew that they would
hate and feel hurt by?

What is the nicest thing you have
ever done for someone else?

How would you spend six hours
with your best friend?

Have you ever organized a large group
of people to do something together?

Where is your favorite place to
sit at home?

What people would you like to weed
out of your life?

You can have one person from any
time in history call you for advice and
follow what you tell him or her to do.
Who would you want it to be?

What would you say to the person you
lost and later found?

Do you confide in someone
on a daily basis?

Did you ever have a physical
fight with a friend?

Do friends call before they stop by?

If you disapproved of a friend's behavior or decision, would you tell him or her?

What new friends have you made?

What frustrates you most about your current relationships?

What do you look for in a friend now?

What relationships are most important to you?

What qualities would your relationships ideally have?

Who is someone you wish you had seen more of as an adult?

How much does it matter that most people like you?

How does your family celebrate Christmas or Hanukkah?

WHAT WOULD YOU DO IF . . .

. . . *someone you love deeply is murdered and you know the identity of the murderer, who is acquitted of the crime? Would you seek revenge?*

. . . *you discovered your best friend is addicted to drugs?*

. . . *you were at a party and people started gossiping about a friend who was not there?*

. . . *your friend and his or her mate have a violent fight in your presence?*

. . . *you feel a distance growing between you and a friend?*

. . . *someone insults a friend to your face?*

. . . *a close friend gets arrested for theft?*

. . . *your best friend has a weight problem?*

Do you remember the dates of your best friends' birthdays?

What was a big misunderstanding you had with a friend?

Who has ever betrayed you?

Would you commit perjury for a close friend?

Who is your best neighborhood friend as an adult?

When you reminisce with friends about wild times, do you have to flash back more than five years?

How do you get the attention of your friends and family?

What relationships should you end altogether?

Do you like mixing with people who are unpredictable and/or nonconformist?

What grabs your attention when someone walks by?

What charity work have you done?

How do you prefer that affection is expressed toward you?

Do you have any friends with severe health problems?

What are two things that help people have a close relationship?

Is there a limit to the number of friends a person should have?

Would you lie to keep a friend
out of trouble?

What volunteer work would you like
to do?

What qualities make a person a
"best friend?"

If your friends or family members were
willing to bluntly and honestly tell you
what they really thought of you, would
you want them to?

What kinds of people do you
like the most?

Would you lie so as not to hurt
someone's feelings?

Do you like constant company
or to be alone at times?

What people have you met on
vacation who have become friends?

Are you more comfortable around
men or women and why?

How did someone once help you
when you were not feeling well?

Do you think you are a good judge
of character?

Have you ever been wrong about
a friend's character?

What social event did you not want
to go to that turned out great?

Who is the kindest person you
have ever known?

Are most of your friends older,
younger, or the same age as you?

What quality do you like most
in a person?

If you could give some of the good in
your life to someone, who would it be?

How do you react when a friend
criticizes you?

Your close friend asks—and genuinely
wants—your opinion on something,
but your opinion is one that he is likely
to find quite painful. Would you tell
your friend the truth?

What makes your best friend
special to you?

What makes someone unforgettable?

What would be the most difficult
thing to forgive someone for?

What is more important to you:
work and accomplishments or friends
and family?

Does other people's ignorance
appall you or can you tolerate it?

What are three good reasons why
someone should have you for a friend?

What are some funny thing(s) that
happened to you and a friend?

What criticism directed at you has been
the most difficult for you to let go of?

Do you hate anyone?

Would you rather be a half hour early
to a party or an hour-and-a-half late?

What was an embarrassing incident
with a good friend?

What games have you played to get on
the right side of people who matter?

Compassion and goodness remind
you of whom?

Do you enjoy or not enjoy big
noisy parties?

How long have you known your
best friend?

Who is someone who encourages you?

What would you do if everyone in
your family forgot your birthday?

What is a characteristic in others
that you admire?

What is the greatest distance you
traveled by car on a family vacation?

Who is your best character witness?

Who is someone who frightened
you and how?

Who would you want in your lifeboat?

Who would you take on a month-long
backcountry camping expedition?

What is the one thing that someone
has said or done that showed his or
her support for you?

What is a particularly dangerous
thing you did with a friend?

Do you have more friends or enemies?

What have you learned from
your enemies?

DO YOU . . .

. . . get embarrassed when people do something special for you?

. . . introduce yourself or wait for others to introduce themselves?

. . . prefer small groups or big parties?

. . . need to be indispensable to family and friends?

. . . prefer being alone or with someone?

. . . prefer to attend big family reunions or school reunions?

. . . have a friend who passed away?

. . . have a friend with a different ethnic background?

. . . know the color of all of your friends' eyes?

I am sorry that I will never again see
_____.

Where did you and your friends spend time as teenagers?

What happens to the family when it is under stress?

What would you like to learn about your family history?

What friends from high school do you stay in touch with?

Do you live in or near the same town you grew up in?

When was a time that peer pressure influenced you and was the outcome positive or negative?

What is the one family value you believe in the most?

If money were not an issue,
what gift would you like to buy
someone in your family?

How do you feel about teenage
marriages?

What is something your father or
mother considered very important?

How forgiving are you when
someone lets you down?

Who would you like to get in contact
with that you have not
spoken to in years?

Who were the major betrayers
in your life, especially those you
were always loyal to?

Talk about "your crowd"—the people
with whom you spend the most time.

Who do you trust more than
anyone in the world?

What is the most selfless thing
you have ever done for someone?

DO YOU . . .

. . . have friendships that have lasted over 10 years?

. . . win people over by telling them what they want to hear?

. . . feel vengeful or forgiving if someone hurts you?

. . . stay in contact with many people from your past?

. . . stay in the background at parties or
put a lamp shade on your head?

. . . take advice from friends?

. . . seek advice from friends?

When you really want to get to know someone, do you tell them?

What kind of people do you like to spend time with?

What do you find interesting about people?

What friends do you still have from your childhood?

What can you do to be a better friend?

Would you sponsor a foreign visitor in your home?

Have you ever had a difficult neighbor?

If you were lonely, who would you seek out?

If someone hurt you terribly and got away with it, would you seek revenge?

Who has been your friend longest and what do you like best about that friend?

How important is it that your friends share your values?

Do you share the same values as your parents?

What are the differences between your mother and your father?

How are you different from your siblings, if you have any?

Who is the most important person in your life?

Are you slow to trust people?

Was there a time when you
could have helped someone and
regret not doing so?

Who is someone you would
describe as a "real character?"

Do you expect a great deal of others?
Of yourself?

Do you remember names
of the people you meet?

Have you ever had a feud with
someone that went on too long?

What person has stayed by
you through thick and thin?

Do you do your share or
more than your share?

Do you like or dislike
throwing parties?

Is your current best friend anything
like your childhood best friend?

Who is your best reference
when applying for a job?

When you fall in love, do your
relationships with friends and
family change?

What things do you display
when friends come to visit?

What would be the perfect party?

What traits do you not like
in other people?

How many times in an average week do you go out socially with your mate; with your friends?

What activities in your community would you like to take part in?

Who is someone you would really like to be friends with?

Who is the funniest person you have ever met and how did you meet?

Who did something for you that seemed insignificant at the time that ultimately had profound impact on your life? What did this person do and how did it impact you?

Do you try to change someone when your opinions differ?

Are you a party person?

What you think about fighting?

Who loves you for who you really are?

Who were your first friends and relationships after college or the military?

Are you quick or slow at making new friends?

What is the strangest name of someone you know?

To whom did you turn for advice as a teenager? Why that person?

Under what circumstances would you lay your life down for a friend?

Have you ever read someone's diary without his or her permission?

What have you learned from friends who
have a different background from you?

What do you and your friends
do together?

What people were unfriendly to
you in the last year?

You are embarrassed when others
_____.

Have you ever looked up an old
friend online?

Did you learn to take yourself less
seriously through your friendship
with someone?

What people have you hurt
that you are sorry about?

For what particular person do you
have the most respect?

How much influence do you think you
have on people?

Do you wish you had more influence
on people than you do?

Are you most attracted to people who
seem fascinated by you?

Is it easy or difficult for you
to make friends?

Whose deaths have moved you
the most?

What three qualities do you require
in a friendship?

You can tell a lot about a person by
_____.

Do you prefer to hang out with people who are like you or who are totally different from you?

Are you a leader or a follower?

Do you have any friends from your parents' generation or older?

Would you rather talk to everyone at a crowded party for a short time or have a significant conversation with two people?

What was the kindest thing a stranger ever did for you?

Would you tell a good friend if they had bad breath?

What would be a fun new way of greeting people?

Are you married?

Do you have kids?

If you do not have kids already, do you want kids?

Do your individual takes on the joys and anxieties of child-rearing complement or contradict each other?

Giving birth: how old is too old?

Would you rather have ten children or none?

What is the scariest thing about parenting?

What should children always be punished for?

Should children be sheltered
from unhappiness?

How would you handle sex education
for your children?

What do you think is the
most difficult thing about being
a teenager today?

How would you react if your
child was homosexual?

What would you find most difficult
to give up as a form of punishment?

What drives you craziest about
children, yours or others?

What special problems do unwed
mothers face?

Do you think it is a problem when
children are born to single parents?

WHO IS . . .

. . . someone you respect and why?

. . . the biggest person you know?

. . . your most eccentric friend?

*. . . the person who can help you negotiate
a path through a crisis?*

. . . someone you wish you had never met?

*. . . one childhood friend you would like to
know what happened to?*

. . . your long-time enemy?

*. . . someone you would like to speak at your funeral?
What would he or she say about you?*

. . . your best friend of the opposite sex?

Would you ever employ a nanny or guardian for your children?

What are your thoughts on how children are raised today?

What is one thing you would like to be sure your children remember?

What part of parenting do you think you could be better at?

What is the single-most important piece of advice you would give a child?

What parenting moment would make you most proud?

Do you believe in not allowing kids to see certain movies and TV shows?

How do you feel about spanking a child?

Tell about an incident with a child in a supermarket or store.

What did/would you name your children?

What should be the earliest age for piercing ears?

What is a parent's greatest accomplishment?

What do you think is the most difficult aspect of being a parent today?

What do you like best about kids, yours or others?

How many children have you planned to have?

What would you like to teach your children about death and dying?

What school or type of school do you want your children to attend?

What was the most important thing that your parents did in raising you that you would like to do for your children?

What qualities of your grandparents and parents would you like your children to have?

What is something you did for your children that you would never have done for anyone else?

What is the greatest lesson a child ever taught you?

What would you like to teach your children about puberty and sex?

Is it harder, easier, or the same to love an adopted child?

At what age do you think children are most difficult?

Would you rather know the sex of your unborn child or be surprised?

Is it possible to be a perfect parent?

What was your proudest moment as a parent?

What do you think about parents having a baby sleep in their bed?

When should you tell a child that there is no Santa Claus?

HOW CAN YOU . . .

. . . make your dad or mom smile?

. . . make more time for the people you love?

*. . . teach your children about the role of money
in life and responsibility?*

. . . discipline children while still showing you love them?

. . . help your children to get along better with other children?

. . . even out the workload between mothers and fathers?

. . . get kids to watch less TV?

What would you do if your baby was born with Down's syndrome or any other developmental disability?

What chores would you assign to children to teach work and responsibility?

What difference is there in satisfaction for parents raising an adopted child?

What is the oldest age that you would want to begin parenthood?

Do adopted children love their adoptive parents as they would have loved their birth parents?

What kind of person do you want your child to marry?

When should a child be told that he or she is adopted?

Do you think adopted children have the right to know their birth parents?

If allowed to make only a fifteen-minute videotape for your kids before you die, what would you say?

What is a good treatment for the
baby blues?

What has the most influence on
today's children?

Do you have nicknames for
your children?

What is something you think you
should tell your children that you are
reluctant to tell them?

What adjustments must be made
by a couple with children?

Have your parents played an
important role in the lives of
your children?

Do you think preschool-age
children suffer if both parents work
outside the home?

Do you have a child who is
most like you?

Do you have a child who is most
like your partner?

Would you let your kid live in
a coed dorm?

At what age should children be
allowed to get their driver's license?

How does family life differ for your
children from the way family life was
for you?

What were the first fully understandable
words your children spoke?

How do you work out differences in
parenting styles?

When has a child inspired you?

What would you do if your teenager stole from you?

What punishment is most appropriate for kids?

Describe what kind of relationship you would like to have with your kids.

Are teenagers being pushed into acting older than they really are?

Do you think that you are/would be a good parent?

What traits do you think are most important to instill in a child?

What TV mom or dad do you think you are most similar to?

What famous person would you like to have a child with?

What things would you want to convey to children to help them along in life?

What makes a child spoiled?

What is worse: overprotective or permissive parents?

Do you think kids watch too much television?

Should men be made to have babies?

What would you like to teach your children about different cultures and races and about people with disabilities?

Would you push your kids to excel at almost any sacrifice?

What are the most difficult things single parents have to face?

What career path would you like your children to enter?

What goes through your mind when you see a newborn child?

Do you like to be around children?

Would you rather encourage your child in the arts or in sports?

Would you discourage your child from developing a talent that may not provide a lot of money?

Your child has talent but wants to quit music lessons because of the hard work; do you relent?

What would you like to introduce and share with your children to help them grow intellectually?

Can you hug kids too much?

What is the most important duty of a parent?

What is one famous quote you want your children to remember?

What is something you think moms will always be better at than dads?

What is the most draining aspect of parenthood?

What is the most fulfilling aspect of parenthood?

WHAT IS THE BEST . . .

. . . stuff your parents taught you about life?

. . . way to deal with someone who has hurt you?

. . . nickname of someone you know?

. . . part of being a parent?

*. . . way to show children that you really love them,
besides hugs and kisses?*

. . . place to raise kids?

Should underage children be allowed
to drink alcohol in their own homes?

What do you think about prodding
unwed dads to admit paternity?

Should men have a say in whether or
not a woman has an abortion?

How does one "shape the will without
breaking the spirit" of children?

What is one thing you would like
to be sure your children remember
about you?

What would be the message
you would like to give your great-
grandchildren?

What are your feelings about putting
to death a handicapped child at birth?

What do you think about aborting a
baby with severe mental retardation?

What did you think when you first
saw your baby(ies)?

How much do you read
to your children?

What would you do if your children
started using drugs?

What type of grandparent
would you be?

If you knew that your child would be
born with a genetic defect and is likely
to die by the age of five, would you
decide to have an abortion?

At what age do you think children
are cutest to observe?

What professional athlete or other
famous person is the best role model
for children today?

What do you think about nursing
a baby in public?

How does TV affects kids' attitudes,
values, and behavior?

What games and activities do you play
with your children?

What toy do kids have that you
would like?

Would you ever adopt a child?

What is your definition of love and
how would you describe it to a child?

What is the most important thing
you would want to teach your kids?

What is something that today
seems impossible to do or achieve
with your children?

What is the ideal age to become
a parent?

What would be the ideal number of children if money was no concern?

What would you like to do for your children's weddings?

What would you do for a kid having a temper tantrum?

Should age sixteen be the age for a driver's license?

What is something you think dads will always be better at than moms?

What influences do we need to protect kids from?

Why do you want to have kids?

What would you do or how do you think you would react if you found out that your child was pregnant or responsible for getting someone pregnant while in high school?

Dangerous kids: how far should we go to keep them in check?

Dating age: how young?

What things would you like to teach your children before they learn it from someone else?

If adopted, would you try to find your birth parents?

When was a time when a child embarrassed you?

Would you want your children to be lawyers?

If you were to have a child right now,
would you rather have a girl or a boy?

What are three things you would
not allow your children to do?

What values do you want to pass
on to your children?

Does your lifestyle undermine
any values you would want your
kids to have?

What is one piece of advice you
would give to a new mother or father?

What kind of life would a child
born to teenage parents experience?

What is something you had to do
that you would not want your children
to ever have to do?

Under what circumstances, if any,
is it okay to hit a child?

How do/would you confront
and discipline your kids?

What makes a great parent?

Fun
& Sport

Anything can be fun if you want it to
be: agree or disagree?

What is the most exciting thing you
have ever done on a dare?

How do you like to go crazy
and have fun?

What is the best clean joke you
have ever heard?

What was the craziest thing you
have ever done in the woods?

What was your best New Year's Eve?

What was your best Christmas
or Hanukkah?

What was your best birthday?

List ten things you like to do for fun.
Were they on your list five years ago?

What would you do if your
TV stopped working?

What team sport do you excel at?

Would you rather skydive
or hang glide?

What physical activity, like jogging,
would you like to begin?

Where would you like to go
surfing and why?

What is the most outrageous thing
you have ever done for money?

What was the first movie you
remember watching on a date
and with whom?

What song best captures an experience or feeling you had?

Who is the sexiest actor and actress?

What are your preferences in music?

What was the last book you read and why did you choose it?

What are you currently reading?

Would you rather put together a 30,000-piece jigsaw puzzle or read a dictionary cover-to-cover?

Have you ever taken art lessons?

If you could have any television program back, not in reruns but in new episodes, which program would it be?

What Trivial Pursuit category do you answer correctly most often?

What are your favorite sports teams, college and professional?

What would you like to be able to create with your own hands?

What subject do you most appreciate in art (e.g., flowers, people, etc.)?

What movie plot did you find most confusing?

During which movie did you laugh the most?

Have you ever performed in public and did you enjoy it?

What is the most fun you have ever had?

Which actress and actor deserve
Oscars who have never won one?

Have you ever played in a band or
sung with a group?

What is your current opinion of TV?

What is the most enchanting music
you have ever heard?

What magazines do you read?

What book do you think should have
been a movie?

What songs do you remember
dancing to?

Do you approve or disapprove
of betting on professional sports?

Would you rather travel with a circus
or a minor league baseball team?

When and where was the last time
you really got to dance?

Do you like to dance?

What was your best golf score
and what was the course like?

What exciting escapades
can you share?

What event in your life would you like
to write a song about?

Is there a common denominator in
your five favorite films?

Have you ever called in a dedication
on a radio show?

WHAT IS YOUR FAVORITE . . .

. . . *aerobic activity?*	. . . *arcade game?*
. . . *Broadway or movie musical?*	. . . *video or computer game?*
	. . . *type of exercise?*
. . . *type of music?*	. . . *concession stand food?*
. . . *sports tradition?*	. . . *water sport?*
. . . *playground equipment?*	. . . *amusement park ride?*
. . . *type of dancing?*	. . . *sport to play?*
. . . *outdoor activity?*	. . . *sport to watch?*

Would you rather browse through a bookstore or a record store?

What movie could you see again and again and again?

Is there usually a TV on in your house no matter what time of day it is?

What movie have you seen several times?

What board game have you had the most luck at?

Is there much music in your house? What kind? Is there much talking?

What category on a quiz show would you choose to get the best chance of winning?

At your worst, you are most like what famous person?

What kind of band do you see yourself fronting?

What subject or story would you like to make a movie about?

What book do you strongly recommend?

What is the value of movie reviews?

What is your opinion of soap operas?

What song do you consider the most romantic?

Is there any value to watching TV?

List five hobbies that sound fun.

Would you sing karaoke in front of strangers?

If you went to a beach and it turned out to be a nude beach, would you stay and go swimming?

Would you rather go hiking or watch TV?

Are you a frequent theatergoer?

Have you ever played a sweepstakes?

Do you like to sunbathe, or do you stay out of the sun?

Have you ever made your own film or video?

Do you enjoy listening to books on tape?

Did you ever perform in a local theater or civic organization show?

Should there be a Miss America contest?

Would you compete in a beauty contest?

What figures do you doodle?

What was the last live performance you saw?

Have you ever been in the studio audience of a talk show?

Would you rather go swimming or shopping?

What, in your opinion, is the most misunderstood song lyric?

What sequel to a movie would you write?

Have you ever written a story about yourself?

Are you a fan of any unusual music or films?

Have you ever invented anything just for fun?

If you could watch only one hour of TV a week, what would you watch?

What singer would you like to sing a duet with?

Do you read but not buy magazines in the checkout lane?

What was your most creative act thus far?

Daily journal: would you write censored or uncensored if you knew future generations would read it?

What movie character did you think was most like you?

Do you sing along when the
"The Star-Spangled Banner" is played?

What is the funniest photo you have
ever taken or seen?

What fan letters have you written?

If you stopped watching TV for a year,
what would you do with the extra time
and what would you miss most on TV?

What was the best end to a football
game you have ever seen?

What would be a good replacement
for TV commercials?

What inanimate object would you
choose to be the latest fad?

What was the most memorable
musical performance you have heard?

DO YOU . . .

. . . enjoy playing games or have to win to enjoy?

. . . consider yourself in or out of shape?

. . . go on the roller coaster at the amusement park?

. . . enjoy rough physical activity?

. . . go to movies more now or in the past?

. . . have music on or appreciate silence most of the time?

. . . watch soap operas?

. . . miss record albums?

. . . enjoy ballet or other dance performances?

. . . play cards?

. . . prefer to read or listen to a book on tape?

. . . enjoy sharing leisure time or prefer to be alone?

What music do you prefer to listen to when you are alone?

What was the last great play or movie you discussed with other people?

Have you ever seen a XXX movie?

What movie set would you have liked to live on?

What musical instruments would you like to learn or improve your performance on?

Poetry: do you like it or not?

Do you prefer clean or dirty jokes?

Do you shop for fun, or only when you need something?

Do you like being on the phone?

What were the last three books you bought?

What photo or picture really moves you?

What movie did you like that everybody else hated?

What is too serious to joke about?

What do you think is funny?

What event(s) did you want to see that you bought scalper tickets for?

What new dance styles would you like to learn?

Do you mark in the books you read and why?

What performer would you most like to see in person?

What dances were popular when you were a teenager?

What type of postage stamp would you design?

"Behind the scenes" look: where would you like to have it?

Do you do crossword puzzles?

What songs do you know by heart?

Do you follow current music or prefer oldies?

What TV shows do your kids watch? What are their favorites now and in the past?

What singer or band do you currently listen to the most?

What effect do commercials have on you?

Do you know ballroom dancing with the right steps?

Have you ever snuck into a second movie at a multiplex?

On what subject(s) would you like to write a book or article?

What things have you made by hand for people?

What would you like to sell in a TV commercial?

What actor most deserves an Academy Award?

Talk about a recent movie you enjoyed.

What album have you listened to the most times and why?

Do you enjoying making or building things?

What famous last words inspired you?

What books have you wanted to read more than once?

Who is an author who has affected you?

Do you support TV and radio public broadcasting?

Have you ever seen the *Rocky Horror Picture Show*?

What new hobbies have you taken up?

What circus act would you like to perform?

Where do you shop the most?

How do you organize your photos?

What was the last really trashy book you read?

What do you do only when you are alone?

Have you ever taken music lessons?

Has a song ever hijacked your brain?

Tell about a joke you played on someone.

What were the last three CDs you bought?

Do you write letters or postcards?

Do you know any limericks?

What was the last movie you cried at?

What would you name your rock band?

Which actor or actress deserves to play you in an *A&E Biography*?

What picture would you like of something?

What song makes you instantly happy?

Do practical jokes amuse or annoy you?

What sound would you miss if suddenly unable to hear it?

Would you miss the printed newspaper and why?

Have you ever walked out of a movie or play and why?

What director do you admire most?

WHAT DO YOU . . .

. . . *like to do on a rainy Saturday or other day off?*

. . . *do to reward yourself when you complete a difficult task?*

. . . *call a perfect evening out with your significant other?*

. . . *do with books you have already read?*

. . . *cut out from newspapers?*

. . . *think of the TV ratings system?*

. . . *think about camping?*

. . . *like to do in a swimming pool?*

What is in your home library?

What specific book(s) would you like to read within the next year?

Do you like doodling and drawing?

Who are the authors whose every book you have read?

If you wrote a book, who would you dedicate it to?

What song could you sing in front of a group?

Do you use TV as company/noise, for specific programs, or as an escape?

What front-row seats would you like to have for a singer or musical group?

Have you ever been in a parade?

What object in a museum do you most want to see?

Do you prefer Wolfgang Mozart or Billy Joel?

What videos would you like in your collection?

What home entertainment gadgets do you use?

Would you rather be on the cover of *Time* or *People* magazine?

What is something you do to relax?

Do you escape via soap operas, mystery novels, or anything trashy?

Would you like to be on a talk show?

If you had two hours to waste on anything, what would you do?

What toast do you make most often?

What movie sound tracks do you own?

Do you watch or look at pornographic videos or magazines?

Do you go on roller coasters at amusement parks?

What hobby makes you feel most relaxed?

Have you ever reread books; what is the criteria for doing so?

How would you rate your karaoke singing ability from 1 to 10?

Do you have a poem memorized?

Would you rather watch a drama or a comedy?

Would you rather watch TV or read a book?

Do you and your mate agree on ways to spend leisure time?

How many hours of TV do you watch per day?

What forms of art have you tried?

If you wrote a children's book, what would be your choice of setting and main character?

Which is better: the book or movie version of _____?

If you started a new talk show, who would be your first guest(s) and why?

Do you prefer surfing the Internet over watching TV?

Do you read science fiction?

How often do you go to the movies?

What artist of today do you think will be remembered 100 years from now?

What music do you play when you are really happy? When you are down?

When do you use a Walkman?

What is your favorite Web site?

Would you rather read fiction or nonfiction?

How many newspapers do you read a week?

What annually televised event is an absolute must-see for you?

In what ways does TV affect your relationships?

What was the most boring movie you ever saw?

What are you uncomfortable with on TV?

Singing alone, what song(s) do you sing?

What is the worst work of art you have ever seen?

Do you prefer quiet or vivid paintings?

What one existing book or movie title defines your life?

What Broadway plays have you seen?

Do you like to watch television alone or with other people?

What magazines do you subscribe to?

What is the funniest bumper sticker you have ever seen?

Do you write letters to the editor?

Has anything you have written ever been published?

Which current celebrities do you think will be remembered in fifty years as legends and why?

Do you like discussing a movie afterward or like to keep the experience to yourself?

Who is the most overrated actor in Hollywood?

CAN YOU . . .

. . . sing well?

. . . do a good imitation of anyone or anything?

. . . whistle?

. . . tell when someone is singing off-key?

. . . name three currently popular musicians or musical groups?

. . . roller skate, ice skate, or in-line skate?

. . . juggle?

. . . do a split?

. . . curl your tongue lengthwise into a taco shape?

Who is the most inspiring famous woman or man?

Describe an article you read recently.

Where would you film an action-adventure movie?

Would you rather see Elvis Presley or John Lennon return from the dead?

What famous person do you resemble the best?

Have you ever had a favorite bar or hangout?

If you could paint anything in the world, what it would be?

What entertainer has the best voice?

If you were paid to write a new book on any subject you wished, what it would be about?

What is your singing ability on a scale of 1 to 10?

Do you color in coloring books?

Where do you like to read?

Who is the most romantic singer?

What is the most albums you have by an artist?

Do you have your own personal Web site?

What is the most timeless toy?

What movie had the most impact on your life?

Do you have a favorite quotation?

Who would you like to play opposite
as leading man or lady?

What would you do on a free
sunny afternoon?

How often do you look at mementos
and keepsakes?

What is your idea of a really
relaxed evening?

What special event would you like a
VIP pass to attend?

What book would you like
to memorize?

Records, CDs, and tapes: are yours
organized alphabetically or by music
type or not organized?

Who is an entertainer everybody
loves but you?

Are you good at trivia questions?

What painting would you like to
"walk into" and "experience"?

What thoughts and feelings come
to mind when you think of "play?"

What proverbs or sayings do
you use often?

What was the most enjoyable
club, league, or team to which
you belonged?

Who is the sexiest male
and female celebrity?

Do you like autobiographies?

Would you rather go to an opera or a county fair?

What is an ideal way to spend a hot Saturday in mid-July?

What is the most embarrassing CD/mp3/tape in your collection?

How long do you think you could go without watching TV?

What is your favorite romantic film?

What celebrities would you like to punch in the face?

What memento of a famous person would you like to have?

What character in what novel would you like to be?

During which movie did you cry the most?

Would you rather listen to a news station or a music station?

Do you enjoy or avoid horror movies?

Do you buy books or borrow them from a library?

Would you rather read a book or listen to music?

What would you do with one week to do anything, all expenses paid?

Do you sing, hum, or whistle often?

What reading material is in your bathroom?

What cartoon character do you most identify with?

How often do you look at old yearbooks?

When was a time you performed in front of an audience?

If you could be either a popular singer or a successful writer, which would you choose and why?

Do you know the words to "The Star-Spangled Banner"?

What comics did you read when growing up?

What is the most recent hobby you took up?

What would be the premise of a novel you would like to write?

What hobby would you like to make into a career?

What famous people do you most enjoy reading about?

If you were an artist, what would be the theme of your drawings or paintings?

What performers did you see in concert when you were young?

Would you rather read 100 pages of the Bible or about medieval politics?

What TV show would you most like to be on?

What is the first work of art you remember creating?

Are you interested in antiques?

What was the last movie you saw?

What leisure-time equipment would you like if space and money were not a restriction?

What movie prop or piece of memorabilia would you like to own?

What piece of music makes you sentimental and what does it remind you of?

Do you keep a sketchbook or diary?

Would you rather see the movie or read the book?

Would you rather be a painter, a writer, or a musician?

What card game are you best at?

What people do you respect for creative achievement?

What musical instrument would you like to be able to play professionally?

What is your favorite computer game?

What fairy tale or children's book character do you relate to?

What new ride or attraction would you design for Walt Disney World?

What how-to instruction book would you like to write?

What is the one CD you would take on a desert island with you?

From whom would you like to receive a letter?

Does it usually take you a long time or short time to read a book?

Should intellectual events be more popular than sports events? Will it ever happen?

What stage name would you choose for your film debut?

How many channels do you need on your television?

What is your ideal hobby? How would it enrich your life?

What artist would you like to commission to create a painting for your home?

Have you ever been a contestant on a game show?

On what TV game show would you like to appear?

WOULD YOU . . .

. . . skydive?

. . . try parachute jumping?

. . . ever pose nude for a photograph taken by someone else?

. . . sit in the front seat of a roller coaster?

. . . sing in front of a large audience?

. . . scuba dive?

. . . swim across the Amazon River?

. . . ride 150 mph in a race car?

What magazine would you like to see on every coffee table in America?

Would you rather write a best seller or be a cover model for a national magazine?

Would you rather climb a mountain or read a good novel?

What sport do you wish was coed?

How often do you exercise?

What recreational game or sport would you like to play with others?

What is your favorite sport in which animals participate?

Do you like hiking?

What were your horseback riding experiences?

Would you rather be the worst player on a championship team or the best player on a last-place team?

What is an activity that makes you feel alive?

When playing sports, do you prefer competing against someone who is worse or better than you?

What was your highest score in bowling?

Would you rather roller skate or ice skate?

Do you like or dislike exercising?

Do you watch regular season games of sporting events or just watch the play-offs and championship games?

What gold medal would you like in your trophy case?

Have you ever caught a fish?

Who is the most courageous athlete you have ever seen or heard of?

Would you rather swim in the ocean or in a pool?

Golf: luck or skill?

Do you think women should directly compete with men in sports?

What is the most exciting sporting event?

What would be the ultimate test of your endurance?

Do you own, rent, or borrow camping equipment?

Where in the world would you like to go hiking?

Which professional sports team would you like to coach and what would you do the first week on the job?

Give a sports cheer or chant you remember.

What should the next Olympic sport be and why?

What type of home exercise equipment have you purchased?

What was an entertainment that ended up being a waste of money?

What sport do you think is the most dangerous and would you try it?

Would you rather fly a kite or jump rope?

Would you rather win by cheating or lose while playing fair?

What was the greatest upset in sports history?

What sporting events do you enjoy more on TV than in person?

Should sports stars be role models?

Would you rather run a marathon or swim five miles?

What do you think about kids taking up extreme sports?

Have you ever ridden a tandem bicycle?

Have you ever fired a gun?

Would you rather water ski or snow ski?

What is one of the sports you really enjoy watching or playing?

Where would you like to ride on a motorcycle?

Do you know any magic tricks?

When was the last time you broke a sweat?

Habits

What things can you do with
your eyes closed?

What is consistently in your garbage?

Do you have a hard time waking
up in the morning?

Do you write down your ideas?

Do you think you are hard
on yourself?

Do you meditate? How often?

Do you use caller ID?

What is something you would like to
do to improve your life?

What are the three most
important things you could do to
improve your life if you exerted
greater self-discipline?

What is your best method
of saving money?

What is your strangest possession?

How do you act in an emergency
situation?

Is there anything irrational that you
continually do?

Where is it difficult to be honest
with yourself?

In what ways are men and women
different in communication?

Do you value your time or waste it?

What type of underwear do you
prefer? Do you care what color it is?

Do you value others' time as much
as your own?

How do you make your life more
complex than it needs to be?

Do you have phobias—real or imagined—
or do you think you have none?

What attitudes and habits did you
have to give up to get through life?

What are you obsessive about
and why?

Over the course of your life,
what have you probably spent more
time pondering than anything else?

How do you handle criticism?

If you were in prison, what would
you do with your time?

In what ways you are creative?

What are your weekend rituals?

Do you snore?

Do you talk in your sleep?

When home alone, do you shut the
door when you use the bathroom?

What is the most difficult habit
you have ever tried to get rid of?

When you cannot sleep, what
do you think about and how do
you try to get back to sleep?

What is under your mattress?

Do you bite your fingernails?

How much water do you drink each day?

What will you absolutely not do in front of another person?

Do you sit outside much in the summer or stay in air conditioning?

What about yourself would you like to always keep the same?

How many alcoholic drinks do you drink in a week?

In which order do you read the newspaper sections?

What is your disposal method for gum?

Do you leave dishes in the sink, clothes on the floor?

Do you tend to blow hot and cold or even in temperament?

What is your daily routine?

What things do you say and do when put on telephone hold?

How do you deal with unwanted calls and solicitors?

What habits have you successfully kicked?

Do you color your hair?

Do you like singing in the shower?

In hot weather, do you use a blanket, sheet, or no covering?

Do you put your right or left sock on first?

Have you ever chewed on things
(fingernails, pens, etc.)?

Do you RSVP or ignore responding?

What are your most common
expressions?

Do you ever try to shock people?

What do you procrastinate about?

Do you think before you speak
or blurt things out?

What kind of praise do you
like to receive?

What kinds of things do you
hate spending money on?

What is the minimum
amount of money you need a
year to support yourself?

Do you want an open seat next
to you on an airplane?

How do you stow your socks?

What is your mechanical aptitude?

ARE YOU . . .

. . . a member of a church or synagogue?
. . . a doer or procrastinator?
. . . well-organized?
. . . high-energy or low-energy?
. . . high-maintenance or low-maintenance?
. . . a hypochondriac?
. . . usually found wearing jeans?

Do you turn off the lights when
you leave a room?

What are your Sunday
morning rituals?

What things are you criticized for?

Do you set your watch exactly,
ahead, or behind?

What side of the bed do you
like to sleep on and why?

What is in your average day's mail?

What is the last thing you do
before you go to bed?

What are your eating habits?

What position do you start sleeping in?

What are your swear words?

How do you acknowledge sneezes?

Do you use an alarm clock?

What does your answering machine
recording say?

Can you snap your fingers?

Can you do a cartwheel?

What do you use for bookmarks?

Do you use a brush, a comb, or both?

How often do you trim your
fingernails and toenails?Have
you ever had a pedicure?

What habit did you pick up
from a relative?

Do you have trouble controlling impulses? Which ones?

Do you always give the real reason when asking somebody to do something for you?

Do you stand or walk on escalators?

WHAT IS YOUR FAVORITE . . .

. . . item of clothing?

. . . machine?

. . . room in your house?

. . . line from a movie?

. . . year of your life?

. . . artist?

. . . speed limit?

. . . actress?

. . . car?

. . . month of the year?

. . . catalog?

. . . cooking implement?

. . . activity in each season: fall, winter, spring, and summer?

. . . cartoon?

. . . Thanksgiving food?

. . . position to start tic-tac-toe?

. . . actor?

. . . ice cream flavor and brand?

. . . gadget?

. . . font?

. . . way to renew your energy?

. . . way to eat ice cream?

. . . art style?

. . . perfume or cologne?

. . . pastime?

. . . breed of cat?

. . . buffet item?

. . . boy's name?

. . . pastry?

. . . breed of dog?

. . . sandwich?

. . . retreat or place of respite?

. . . color?

. . . take-out food?

. . . Elvis Presley song?

. . . time to study?

. . . fast-food restaurant?

. . . nickname or alias?

. . . tool?

. . . temperature?

Would you rather be woken up by music or by an alarm?

In what conditions do you prefer to sleep?

What do you sleep in?

How would you like to spend most of your time?

What do you often dream of?

Do you like or dislike spicy food?

Do you read the freshness dates on grocery store products?

What do you like to snack on between meals?

Do you watch what you eat or eat what you want?

Do you sample others' food?

Would you rather eat a candy bar or piece of fruit?

Do you buy organic food?

Do you feel that organic food is better for you than regular food?

What are your personal staples (i.e., food you keep around all the time)?

Why are you not a vegetarian or not a meat-eater?

What is your drink (alcoholic)?

What do you put ketchup on?

What foods do you eat that you know you should not?

What was one of the most unusual
meals you have ever eaten?

Do you use a hair dryer or
air-dry your hair?

Are you eating right?

Do you rinse out toothpaste remains
in the sink?

What Web sites do you go
to everyday or fairly often?

What are your waking-up habits?

What are the first thoughts that
go through your mind the moment
you wake up?

Are you an extrovert or an introvert?

Do you squeeze or roll the toothpaste
tube from the middle, bottom?

How often do you use mouthwash
and which kind do you like?

In what order do you put
on your clothes?

Are you generally on-time, early,
or late-arriving?

Do you have an organized wallet?

What are some ways to stop biting
your fingernails?

What is a routine you remember
from your childhood?

Do you ask for and/or accept help?

Does anyone you know have a
particularly annoying habit?

What is one personality trait you have tried hardest to change in yourself?

Are you a light/deep/average sleeper?

What elements would a picture of your typical day include?

What is a habit you picked up during your working years?

Do you put down the toilet seat?

Are you a picture taker or forgetter of the camera?

What is your placement of return address and stamp on an envelope?

Do you sleep with one or two pillows?

How do you react when things do not go as planned?

What do others think your worst habit is and what do you think your worst habit is?

Do you lock the front door, leave the lights on, or use other security measures?

Are you getting enough sleep?

Do you replace the toilet paper roll immediately?

How often do you shave, what is your method of choice, and where do you shave?

What do you read and why?

What things do you check at night before going to bed?

What are your nighttime rituals?

Do you hoard magazines?

Do you talk particularly fast or slow?

What bargain items do you look for?

With books: do you read the last page first? Do you skip ahead?

Do you finish every book you start?

What checks do you write every month that you hate to sign?

What charities do you give to?

Do you like buying things?

Do you usually pay your bills on time?

Does advertising significantly influence your buying decisions?

What department store most suits your needs and tastes?

If you could afford it at this moment, what would you buy?

What brand names do you buy and swear by and that you would never switch from?

Have you ever played bingo for money?

Have you ever visited a casino?

Have you ever bet on a horse race?

Have you ever bought a state lottery ticket?

What was the last bet you won?

Do you buy anything in bulk?

WHAT IS THE . . .

. . . first thing you turn to in the newspaper?

. . . direction and process of your teeth-brushing?

. . . first thing you do when you wake up in the morning?

. . . number of laundry loads you do in a week?

. . . last thing you see before you close your eyes at night?

How much cash do you normally carry with you?

What percentage of your earnings do you save?

Do you write with expensive or cheap disposable pens?

Do you take a shower or bath every day, less, or more often?

Do you floss regularly, sporadically, or not at all?

What mirrors do you look in every day?

Do you fall asleep with the TV or radio on?

Do you have special rituals to make yourself fall asleep?

Do you use your computer more for work or play?

How long does your shower last?

When was the last time you made an international telephone call?

Do you regularly read the obituaries?

What habits or mannerisms of yours remind you of your mother or father?

Are you patient or impatient while waiting for something?

Do you eat meals at the same time every day?

What are your most compulsive habits?

What habits have you not been able to break?

Are you an early bird or a night owl?

What are your annoying habits?

What things do you save and recycle?

What time do you go to sleep?

Are you considered a regular at any eating establishment?

Do you read in the bathroom?

How long do you keep bad habits from a new partner?

Do you use a night-light or no light?

What do you do with advertisement cards in magazines?

What letters have you saved and from whom?

What is one of the simple pleasures of life you truly enjoy?

What excuses do you use or have used to get out of dates or appointments?

Do you use swear words frequently or infrequently?

WHAT IS YOUR SIGNATURE . . .

. . . adjective?

. . . one-word answer?

. . . dish?

. . . saying and why it is important to you?

. . . scent?

. . . topic of conversation?

. . . greeting?

. . . sign-off?

Do you establish routines?

What things do you do between turning off the alarm and walking out the door?

What do you do while you are on the phone?

Do you fold your undergarments or just throw them in a drawer after washing them?

How much time do you spend reading each day?

About what time do you get up on an average weekday morning?

What is your main sleep position?

How do you react when short of sleep or under stress?

What is your most recent lie?

Are you cleanliness-compulsive
or do you not mind dirt?

Do you work out?

How do you open the mail?

What are the items in your wallet?

What do you do during a power
outage?

Do you seek out new experiences
every day?

What is in your medicine cabinet?

Do you pick your nose?

Do you give up your seat to others?

What is a habit you picked up during
your earliest years?

How long do you brush your teeth?

Have you ever tried to persuade
somebody to give up a habit?

Are you fanatically tidy, extremely
untidy, or somewhere in-between?

What do you do most frequently
when you think no one is looking?

Do you tie and untie shoes
or slip them on and off?

Do you button shirts top-to-bottom
or bottom-to-top?

What habits are you proud of?

Have you ever been part
of an intervention?

DO YOU PREFER . . .

. . . to watch or participate?
. . . malls, catalog shopping, or the Internet?
. . . a bath or shower?
. . . to talk to people by telephone, in person, or by e-mail?
. . . odd or even numbers?
. . . typing or writing in longhand?

Have you ever participated in a twelve-step program?

Do you steal sheets or covers or have them stolen from you?

What is the trustworthiness of consumer marketing reports?

What do you complain about most?

Why do you think that people have such a hard time quitting a bad habit?

Do you lose things or know where everything is?

Do you follow the news as closely on the weekends as you do during the week?

What is your average night's sleep on a weeknight?

What are your addictions?

How often do you brush your teeth?

What habit would you like to start?

Have you ever stolen anything?

How do you pick a doctor?

What do you think about when
you daydream?

On what days of the week do
you do certain chores?

If you could change the balance
between work, family, and play, in
what way would you?

When was the last time you
were really drunk?

Are you right-brained or left-brained?

What time do you like the sun to set?

What one personality trait would
you like to have?

How do you act when you want
to avoid doing something?

Which shoe do you put on first?

You open mail in what order?

Do you shave your legs and
underarms?

Do you wear makeup all the time or
only sometimes?

Is it hard for you to sit still or are you
mainly sedentary?

What things do you do in the same
order each day and how do you feel if
you skip a step or miss a day?

Are you at the computer or TV more?

Do you pick up after yourself?

Do you use deodorant, antiperspirant, or both?

Are your books alphabetized or categorized?

Do you like or dislike foreigners?

Do you try to save an extra seat for yourself on the train or in a movie?

Are your pets allowed to ride in the car, lie on the furniture, go visiting with you, go on family vacations, be fed at the table?

Do you make the bed daily?

Where do you usually get most of your news about what is going on in the world today?

Do you gamble regularly?

Do you play the lottery?

Are you a conventional dresser? Always?

Have you ever gone to a psychologist or therapist?

Do you buy brand-name clothes?

Do you take any type of medication when you come down with a cold?

What do you have done at the beauty or barber shop and how often?

What daily health habit would you like to develop and be disciplined about?

How often do you go to the dentist? To the doctor?

Have you ever worn uncomfortable
shoes because they looked good?

Do you give money to
homeless people?

What do you wish for on pennies
in a wishing well?

What do you do to decrease
your taxes?

Do you enjoy writing? What type
of writing? Do you show it to others
or keep it private?

In what order do you keep your
currency in your wallet?

Do you buy products specifically
for "green"/environmentally friendly
advertising and/or packaging?

Have you ever switched price tags
in a store?

Are you careful or careless with money?

What you would invest in if you had
the money?

Do you ever take sleeping pills?

What do you do to stop hiccups?

What topic puts you to sleep more
quickly than any other?

Have you had a recurring dream
throughout life?

What usually goes through your
mind just before you fall asleep?

Are you easy or difficult to
get along with?

WHAT IS YOUR USUAL . . .

. . . breakfast?
. . . lunch?
. . . dinner?
. . . bedtime?
. . . dream at night?
*. . . wish when you blow out candles on
your birthday cake?*

What is a dream you have had
more than once?

What one object would you grab if
your house was on fire?

Do you like or dislike schedules?

Do you dream in color or black
and white?

Do you know when to accept your
measure of responsibility for a bad
break?

How much time a day do you spend
in front of some kind of screen?

How do you channel frustration into
a nondestructive activity?

Are you good or bad at finishing things?

Do you have a fear of insects?
Which kind?

What can and will you kill?

What is the strangest thing you save?

What is likely to cause you to "blow up?"

What scent would you like to
bottle as a perfume?

Do you tend to lose things?

Is your house very neat or
somewhat messy?

Do you do what you say you
are going to do?

Would you rather wear tight
or loose pants?

Do you sleep naked or in pajamas?

What do you do when you
catch a cold?

Have you ever hitchhiked?

Have you ever picked up hitchhikers?

Where would you go if you wanted to
spark your creativity?

What jewelry do you like to wear and
what do you not like to wear?

What are the landmarks in your
life: certain buildings, stores, things
you see every day?

What do you see from your
bedroom window?

At what temperature do you best
like the house?

Do you sometimes drink more
than you should? When?

What self-improvement techniques
have you experimented with?

What talents or skills of yours are
now rusty from lack of practice?

What time of day do you feel
most creative?

What smell makes you feel safe
and cared for?

Were you ever in trouble
with the law?

Can you wiggle your ears?

Are you right- or left- handed?

What things physically drain
you on most days?

What keys do you have on your
key chain?

What is something (not immoral
or controversial) that if you did it,
it would shock everyone?

Have you ever ground your teeth?

Does your mind ever go blank in
the middle of doing something?

Are you quick or slow at making
a witty reply?

Do you ever turn a crisis into
a story you tell, with you as the star?

When do you feel impatient?

What task do you put off until
tomorrow most often?

What things do you always
make time for?

Love & Sex

How often have you fallen in love?

Do you believe in love at first sight?

What was the worst pick-up line you have ever heard?

Physically, what do you look for in a man or woman?

How do you settle differences in your relationship?

Who was a memorable adolescent sweetheart?

Would you ever want to change your gender—at least for a day?

What wedding did you object to or wanted to object to?

What would you like to do with your mate that you have never done?

Which areas of your past are most important for you to discuss with a fiancé(e)?

What drives you craziest about your partner?

Is fidelity obsolete or coming back?

Do you think it is possible for a person to be truly asexual?

How old were you when you first had sex?

Describe the person to whom you lost your virginity.

What is your longest grudge?

In what ways have you changed since getting married?

What is the appropriate age for having sex the first time?

What is the greatest gift you have to offer your partner?

What do you enjoy or dislike most about having a committed relationship?

Do you wish you had slept with more or fewer people?

Which do you find more acceptable: older men with young women or young men with older women?

Do you believe in kissing on the first date?

What was the best pick-up line you have ever heard?

How old were you when you married?

What clothes do you think are sexy?

Does your mate trust you?

What is your sexiest feature?

What was your best sexual experience?

What person did you unsuccessfully pursue over a long period of time?

When are your relationships the happiest?

WHAT IS YOUR FAVORITE . . .

. . . love story?

. . . first-date story?

. . . blind-date story?

. . . love song and the lyrics in the song you like best?

. . . type of kiss?

. . . kind of date?

. . . indecent proposal?

What heroic things have you done for love?

What are loving ways to say "I'm not in the mood?"

What would someone have to do to make you fall in love with him or her?

The best part about marriage is _____.

Can people be in love with each other even if they do not want to stay together as life partners?

Does your marriage embody the principles you each consider key?

When my partner is happy, I am happy: true or false?

Who makes most of the decisions in your relationship?

Do you think that your significant other would say you are good in bed?

What are two things that are appealing about men (or women)?

What would you do if you found out
your partner was faking orgasms?

Who were the one(s) that got away?

What would you say to your latest
ex if you saw him or her again?

Who is a person you regret
sleeping with?

What person did you successfully
pursue in a short amount of time?

How long does it usually take before
you will sleep with someone?

What could you do, give up, or
compromise to improve your
relationship with your mate?

What are the best reasons for
getting married?

What was the most unbelievable
date you ever had?

When is it hardest for you to give or
receive hugs?

Does marriage expand or restrict
your sense of the possibilities in life?

Do you believe it is possible to be with
one person for the rest of your life?

Do you think you are good in
bed sexually?

What astrological signs are you most
and least compatible with?

Do you believe in mandatory
premarital counseling to help
lower the divorce rate?

What terms of endearment
do you use?

When you met your mate:
what did you first notice, like best,
want to know more about?

What three qualities are most
important in someone you date?

What would you do if you caught your
spouse having sex with someone else?

Would you rather die before
or after your partner?

What attracts you the most to a
prospective partner?

What do you think about
premarital sex?

With whom have you had the
most intimate conversation?

Marriages and significant long-term
relationships are meant to _____.

When discussing your love life,
do you tend to exaggerate, understate,
or be factual?

Things would be a lot better if only
my partner would _____.

Do you feel comfortable introducing
old lovers to a current one?

What is the best place to make love
other than a bed?

Two days alone with your mate:
how would you like to spend
them and where?

Can you remember the name of your first boy/girlfriend?

Did you ever fall in love with someone that your best friend or sibling was dating?

What is your biggest complaint about your mate?

When has jealousy affected your relationship with someone?

Are you surprised or flattered by what your mate says about you?

Did you date much or little?

What boy/girlfriends do you remember most vividly?

Do you stay in touch with your exes?

What are the most romantic cities?

What do you like to do after making love?

Is there a hole in your life, that is, a person you feel you should have been with?

HAVE YOU . . .

. . . ever had sex in a dangerous place?

. . . ever been in love with more than one person at a time?

. . . ever been divorced?

. . . ever flirted via e-mail?

. . . ever tried online dating?

. . . ever fallen in love by e-mail alone?

. . . ever tried speed dating?

Whose marriage do you admire?

In your current relationship, who is more emotionally stable?

What do you think determines sexual orientation: nature or nurture?

What is something someone said or did that you found very unattractive?

Do you consider yourself a romantic?

What TV series or movie best describes your love life?

What makes love exciting for you in your relationship now?

What idiotic things have you done for love?

Who is a person you regret not sleeping with?

When a couple breaks up, does it mean one of the partners has failed?

What do you think the most frequent sexual complaint of couples is?

What was the best date you have ever had with your mate?

Have you ever wondered what friends or colleagues are like in bed?

How has the role of romance changed in your life over the years?

Define "commitment." What is the scariest thing and the most rewarding thing about commitment?

Do you like to flirt and think that flirting is okay and romantic?

What is a fulfilled sexual fantasy of yours?

What is the longest time you have gone without sex as an adult?

What is the best word to describe your current love life?

Tell a honeymoon story.

What are the ways you like love to be shown to you?

How old were you on your first date and what was the experience like?

What happened to your first love?

Have you ever broken a date to go on a date with someone else?

Define the perfect marriage.

Describe the perfect divorce.

What two qualities are most important in a marriage partner?

What is something someone said or did that you found extremely attractive?

How do you talk about the person in your life when you are not with them?

What do you think about arranged marriages?

Did you/would you live with someone before marriage?

Is marriage an outdated institution?

What is love and what makes love last?

What fragrance reminds you of someone you were once with?

Should the law punish lovers who lie?

What would you like to receive or do for your anniversary this year?

What person would you like to do a love scene with?

Why do people try to change each other?

What is the single most important piece of advice you would offer to a person of the opposite sex?

Define "intimacy."

What was the largest age difference you had in a relationship?

Do you think more, fewer, or the same number are cheating on a spouse compared to five or ten years ago?

When was your first blind date?

Who was your first love?

How do you feel about sex and nudity in a movie with a relatively new date or friend? With your spouse?

What was your honeymoon spot and why did you pick it?

Do you think you argue with your significant other frequently?

What people do you love?

Do you have a belief that love depends on good sex?

Are you ever too old to fall in love?

Should couples have a prenuptial agreement?

Describe the first time you fell in love.

Where would you go to meet people if you were single?

Would you rather know that your spouse had a one-night stand or never find out?

Is there one perfect mate for everyone?

What do you think about marrying someone of a different race, nationality, or religion?

What words would you love to have whispered in your ear?

WOULD YOU TRY . . .

. . . an online dating service?

. . . participating in a mate-swapping party?

. . . participating in an orgy?

. . . S&M?

. . . try a covenant marriage?

. . . something new if your partner asked?

. . . sex in an airplane?

. . . to donate sperm or eggs to someone you are not in a romantic relationship with?

What about love makes you afraid?

In your relationship, who is in charge of interior design?

What constitutes betrayal?

What are two things that are not appealing about men (or women)?

Who was your unrequited love(s)?

What was your first year of marriage like?

Describe your first kiss.

Is there a chemical reaction to love?

How much absence should there be in a relationship to make the heart grow fonder?

How can we be more loving to one another?

What is your anniversary date?

Would you rather fall in love and lose that person or never fall in love at all?

How long does it takes a couple to work things out between them?

Where did you get engaged and how was the marriage proposal made?

Do you purchase condoms in stores or by mail/Internet?

What would you change in a current relationship and why?

What is the difference between you and your partner that you value the most and one that you consider problematic?

Do you try for the perfect union coupled with perfect autonomy?

What is your general opinion about married people cheating?

What person in your life is the best example of love?

When picking a life partner, do you follow your head or your heart?

Are you faithful?

Would you rather pick out your engagement and/or wedding ring or be surprised by your fiancé(e)?

How much love are you comfortable with?

What is the hardest adjustment in marriage?

How do you flirt and get someone's attention?

Do you consider yourself a good flirt and like it?

Do you flirt with others even if you are in a relationship?

Who starts more arguments, your significant other or you?

When was a time when someone held your hand?

What is the point of marriage?

In a relationship, how much
independence do you need?

What illusion did you have
about married life that you
realized was not true?

What are three wishes you have
for your marriage?

What do you enjoy most and least
about married life?

What was a funny thing you
did to your mate?

Using A, B, C, D, F grading,
what grade would you give your
current relationship?

What are the major factors in
a lasting relationship?

When you are attracted to
someone, do you like to be the
cat or the mouse?

In your opinion, are there any
other reasons for marriage than love?

What traits do you require
in a partner?

When or how did you know you
were truly in love with your mate?

Does a marriage have a better
or worse chance at succeeding if
the people live together first?

How much does your mate's
appearance matter to you?

In your relationship, who is
in charge of financial investing?

In your relationship, who generally pays when you go out to a restaurant or movie?

What is essential in a happy marriage or relationship?

Do you and your mate come from similar backgrounds (e.g., education, social status, family income, etc.)?

What is the most planning you have ever put into a romantic event?

What was your best date in high school?

What is one thing you wish your mate would do more often?

What three qualities would your ideal relationship have?

In what ways do you take your mate for granted?

Do you wish you had received premarital counseling?

Where would you like to go on your first or second honeymoon?

Describe your wedding(s)—or the one you would like to have.

What is the biggest misconception about marriage?

How often do you do romantic things for your partner?

Have you ever been to a marriage counselor or therapist with your mate?

How can one keep from becoming too dependent on one's loved one?

WHAT IF . . .

. . . your significant other passed away; would you actively seek a partner after an appropriate mourning period?

. . . you were in love with someone but they wanted to stay friends; could you do it?

. . . you went on a honeymoon; where would you go?

. . . you love someone; how often should you say it?

. . . your boy/girlfriend was caught with a prostitute; would you dump him or her?

. . . love makes the world go round; what does lust do?

. . . one partner wants more sex than the other; how can it be worked out?

. . . your marriage ended; how did it happen?

. . . you had to do it over; would you marry the same person?

. . . you found out that your significant other had an abortion; would it affect how you felt about that person?

. . . a man asks a woman to dinner; should he pay?

. . . your partner was diagnosed HIV positive; would you continue your relationship?

What type of wedding ceremony and reception did you have or what type do you dream of?

Have you ever bought or sought out any type of pornography?

What was the hardest relationship you have ever been in?

What is the worst and best thing an ex-lover has ever done to you?

What made love exciting for you in the beginning of your relationship?

What surprises have you thought up for people you love?

Who were the big crushes of your life: movie stars, singers, real people?

People can show their love to me by _____.

Is labor equally divided in your relationship?

What person did you pursue over a long period of time?

What constitutes a good sexual relationship?

The hardest part about marriage is _____.

What gifts from your mate meant the most to you?

What was your last relationship like?

Does a woman have the right to get pregnant even if her partner has said he or she does not want a child?

Must love and sex go together?

Have you ever had an affair?

Have you ever had a one-night stand?

Would you feel comfortable about your significant other not wearing his or her wedding ring?

Are there any parts of the body that you dislike touching or having touched?

Do you worry about whether your dreams can accommodate your mate's and vice versa?

What have you learned about your partner that you did not know in your first six months together?

What is one wedding tradition you would change or eliminate?

What music do you like to listen to while making love?

What is the farthest distance you traveled to be with someone you desired?

Good loving is _____.

What is best thing about starting a new relationship?

What is the worst thing about starting a new relationship?

Do you believe in covenant marriage to help lower the divorce rate?

In your relationship, who is in charge of vacation planning?

Are you possessive or jealous by nature?

What is your favorite and least favorite time of day to make love?

What is your image of the ideal man or woman?

How would you break off a relationship where you lost interest?

What are the advantages and disadvantages of arranged marriages?

Do you know anyone who is in an arranged marriage?

Do you have strong emotional needs?

How many hugs do you need a day?

What is an important lesson you learned from a breakup?

Who was your first steady boy/girlfriend?

Do you prefer ordinary sex?

Who is the most romantic couple you know for real and in movies/TV?

What was the worst heartbreak you have ever experienced?

Why do so many marriages fall apart today?

How can long-range compatibility be determined?

What is the best cure for lovesickness?

Describe your ideal mate.

Who is someone you could imagine yourself being with the rest of your life?

What is one thing you keep telling your mate?

What is a saying about women or men that you believe is true?

What is the typical reason you end a relationship?

Would you have an affair if you could definitely get away with it?

Have your expectations of
your relationship been surpassed
or disappointed?

What is the best and worst
thing that has happened with
your current partner?

How many times have you
felt you would not recover from
a broken heart?

What is one of the best ways for
someone to express his or her love
for you?

What is your favorite sexual fantasy?

What is the most romantic weather?

Who was the last person you said
"I love you" to?

What are turn-ons and turn-offs
to you?

What was the most perverted
situation you were ever in?

What is your strongest sexual asset?

Would requiring couples to have
counseling save many marriages?

Should you marry for love or money?

Is income a consideration in
choosing a mate?

How often do you think of sex
or romance?

Which do you enjoy more:
sex or money?

How many different sexual partners have you had in your life?

People should not marry before what age?

What are the characteristics of a good marriage?

What love relationships did you have in college?

When you are in love, you need _____.

With your first love, who broke whose heart?

Who is smarter, you or your significant other?

What does a woman or man need most from a husband or wife?

What lesson of love took you the longest to learn?

What are three things you love doing with your mate?

In your relationships, do you make most of the decisions?

What was the first impression you had when you met your mate?

When is the right time in a new relationship to have sex?

Do you believe soul mates meet by accident or by destiny?

Do you like a peaceful or hectic life?

If an activity does not result
in progress toward a goal, is it
a waste of time?

What makes you blush?

What compliments do you receive
on a regular basis?

If you did not have commitments
to others, how would you live your
life differently?

What have you not had enough
of in your life?

Is your life moving ahead, backward,
or is it on hold?

What is the greatest goal you want
to achieve within the next five years?

What is something you believed
for a long time that you do not
believe anymore?

Do you think helmets should be
mandatory for motorcycles and
bicycles - for kids and/or adults?

What are three things that you
are optimistic about?

What are three things that you
are pessimistic about?

What are some of the phone calls
that changed your life?

What would you do if you
earned $100,000 a day? How
would your life change?

. . . honesty is always the best policy?

. . . it is possible to live with no regrets?

. . . it is a good idea to always trust your gut?

*. . . the good things in life are either immoral,
illegal, fattening, or unhealthy?*

. . . that one determined person can change the world?

. . . that life is ultimately fair?

. . . you look younger than/older than/exactly your age?

. . . we will be attacked by a nuclear missile?

Would you rather live in Los Angeles
or New York City?

Would you feel comfortable
moving to a city where you do not
know the language well?

What can you guarantee
about yourself?

How do you think the world will
look in 25, 50, 75, 100 years?

What is your greatest talent?

How can you further develop
your talents?

What is something you truly
appreciate or enjoy doing that most
others probably do not care for?

Which do you like best about yourself:
appearance, personality, or intellect?

What was the greatest peer
pressure you felt as an adult?

Are you jealous of other
people's success?

What legacy would you like to leave?

What is something you feel too
young to do?

What parts of your life do you
feel you control and how much of
your life is beyond your control?

Do you like or dislike change?

How close to contentment are you
in your life right now?

What was the most anti-establishment
thing you ever did?

What needs to change for you
to have greater contentment?

What is the most beautiful man-made
object?

Define "hope."

What continually robs you from
appreciating or enjoying the moment?

What are five things you are
grateful for?

What worries you the most?

Is there something you feel too
old to do?

If you had massive energy, how would
you put that energy to work?

What would you do if you met your
exact double?

Do you try innovations or stick to tested methods?

What is something you have dreamed of doing for a long time?

What are the most positive changes you have seen in your lifetime?

What are the most negative changes you have seen in your lifetime?

What would you do if you had $500 to spend on anything?

How do you feel when someone teases you?

What public figure has inspired you?

What could you do, change, or eliminate to help simplify your life?

What is the most precious thing you have lost?

Do you hold stronger opinions than most people?

What is the most beautiful word in the English language?

Do you state your opinions with vehemence?

Where would you move tomorrow if you could, and why?

What is the stupidest thing you have ever done?

What is your ideal living environment?

How much responsibility do you take
for your own problems?

In what areas of your life do you
need long-term solutions rather
than quick fixes?

What was a decision you made
in an instant that gave you a lifetime
of heartache?

Can you confess three tiny faults
and a giant one?

What bothers you most about
your life?

Who is one of the luckiest people you
know, and why?

What is one thing about your life now
that you would not change?

What horrendous blunder did you
make in the past year and what did
you learn from it?

What do you need changed in your life
before you can have more fun?

You love it when people ask
you _____.

I am unhappy with myself when _____.

Is it essential that you succeed in life?

Do you approve or disapprove
of casino gambling on Indian
reservations?

Do you know someone whose
life or personality has been changed
by money?

Do you find it hard or easy to say "no" to a salesperson?

What is your view on selling personal items?

Do you feel comfortable selling anything?

Does legalized gambling encourage people who can least afford to squander their money?

Have you ever been audited by the IRS?

In what circumstances do you feel most susceptible to temptation?

How do you minimize temptation in your life?

What kind of person would you like to be?

Where does honesty work well in your life?

If you had to kill your own food, would you become a vegetarian?

Are you sensitive to the pairing of wine and food?

If you opened a restaurant, what would the house specialty be?

No electricity: how would you manage and what would be different?

How do you deal with things you cannot change?

How did you feel each time you changed homes?

Architecturally, what kind of house do you prefer to live in?

Tell about the time when you were the coldest, the hottest.

What do you like most about your home?

Describe your decorating style.

Which would you choose: to be the most attractive, the most athletic, or the smartest kid in your class?

When you are happy, you need _____.

In general, do you live for today or plan for tomorrow?

Do you agree "life begins at forty?"

What would you like to be doing in twenty years?

What is your most treasured memory?

What is a word for which you have always needed a synonym?

How much responsibility do you have in your life, positive and negative?

What do you think the next ten years of your life will be like?

What self-limiting thoughts or fears would you like to overcome?

How and when do you think that the world will come to an end?

What do you think the world will be like 100 years from now?

If you could change anything in the world's history, what would it be?

For what one activity would you like to regain the hours you have lost doing it?

What significant social change would you like to see happen in your lifetime?

Do you hesitate to answer strangers' questions?

What scares you?

What is your worst nightmare and how often do you have nightmares?

Which worries you more: financial or physical security?

What will and will you not compromise on?

What do you carry to protect yourself? In what other ways do you protect yourself?

Where have you experienced joy in your life?

What do you hate most?

What do you never seem to find time for?

Why do you get up in the morning?

What do you expect each day to bring you?

Do you live in the moment, dwell on the past, or dream about the future?

What has been the most difficult decision or series of decisions where your integrity was at risk?

What daily activity do you treasure more than any other?

Is it possible that certain difficulties require bending, giving in, and even allowing yourself to feel overwhelmed?

In what ways do you express anger?

What is your most prevailing thought?

Do you like snow?

What special places do you go to think things out?

How you would like to change your outer life?

WOULD YOU RATHER . . .

. . . be a student or an employee?

. . . be known for your intelligence or your personality?

. . . live a life of luxury or be known for your generosity?

. . . be 7'2" or 4'2"?

. . . be very good looking or very smart?

. . . be a star and die at forty-two or live to ninety without any fame?

. . . have the power to fly or to disappear?

. . . live safely and longer or go hog wild and live a shorter time?

. . . get a shot from a doctor or get a filling from the dentist?

. . . go blind or deaf?

. . . be President of the United States or the world's richest person?

What things were you once afraid of, but are no longer?

Do you ask questions like a reporter but cringe when the conversation turns back to your life?

Which of life's mysteries are you most curious about?

If you could own the world's largest collection of anything, what would it be?

What superhero powers would you like to have?

Of all the things someone could say about you, what would make you feel the best?

What did you once find frightening that no longer scares you?

What things do you avoid thinking about?

Ten years from today, what will you wish you had done now?

What is something you would like to do that you are not allowed to do?

How do you picture the end of the world?

What is one key thing you could do to produce a quantum leap in your personal life?

How do you view failure? What were important failures for you?

Where do you have immense patience and very little patience?

Do you enjoy the attention of crowds?

How would you rate your public
speaking ability: poor, fair, good,
or exceptional?

What are some big things that
make you happy?

If you were to perform an act of
grace, what would it be?

Can you manage life situations as
easily as most people?

What gives you a feeling of
abundance in life?

Do you enjoy reminiscing
about the past?

When are some times you have had
low self-esteem?

What percentage of the things that
you worry about actually happen?

I feel alone when _____.

Are you an optimist or a pessimist?

Can you make up excuses easily?

List ways in which these things
have had a negative impact on your
life: alcohol, drugs, sex, work, money,
food, family, and friends.

Where is apathy most present in
your life?

Have you ever considered suicide,
even fleetingly?

What are five reasons not to kill yourself?

What is something you would be tempted to do if you knew you would never be found out?

When you accomplish something, do you make sure everyone knows, or do you keep your success to yourself?

What is something you found out that you wish you never knew?

What three wishes do you have for your genie in a bottle?

What is funny about yourself that makes you smile when you think about it?

What are three expectations you have of yourself?

What are you proudest of about yourself?

What do you get enthused about?

Have you tried breaking the what-shall-I-do logjam by taking one step, any step?

What is your need for privacy?

How much do you care about your personal space?

What emotion do you seem to experience the most?

What is the greatest amount of emotional pain you have endured?

If your life has not gone where you thought it would, was it your actions that held you back or your thinking?

What things do you think you cannot live without?

What activities would you do if you were not so afraid?

How can you relate a recent dream to a current problem?

How do you behave when you feel depressed and what do you need most at that time?

What things, people, or activities give you peace of mind and restore you?

How do people know you are angry?

What is one thing you would like forgiveness for?

Is everything a drama with you?

What do you continually get away with?

What are three sounds that disturb you?

How can you tell when people are really listening to you?

What struggles or weaknesses in your life have brought you the greatest frustration?

What is a recent fad you admit to trying?

What is the worst thing that could happen to you if you took a risk and failed?

COULD YOU ACCEPT . . .

. . . being in a wheelchair?

. . . being blind?

. . . being deaf?

. . . losing your sense of taste?

. . . losing your sense of smell?

. . . the death of a parent?

. . . a new religion?

. . . the betrayal of a best friend?

. . . being sent to a psychiatric center?

. . . being sent to a nursing home?

What is the best thing that could happen if you took a risk and succeeded?

What was the last significant crossroads in your life?

How do you want your obituary to read?

What is the most exhilarating experience you have ever had?

What bitterness do you have in your soul?

What promises do you keep making to yourself?

What do you need most right now: faith, love, hope, or peace?

In what ways could you be less selfish?

What do you want your last
words to be?

What consistently worries you
each day?

Anticipation or the real thing,
what is better?

Does what we say to each other make
a difference in our self-confidence?

What do you tell yourself when you
are panicking?

What is something you wish you never
had to worry about again?

In a film about your life, who would
play the main characters?

Would you like to disappear for a long
period of time?

What is a symbol that inspires you?

What kind of person do you want to
be and how do you need to change?

What are the things you must do
before you die?

How has experience determined your
attitudes and beliefs?

How can you stay one step ahead?

What would you like to let go of?

What is the most interesting question
anyone ever asked you?

What is your vision for the future?

Do you like your birthday or dread it?

Do you think that only the unlucky or unworthy suffer defeat?

Three months alone on an island: what would you take besides essentials for survival?

Is stubbornness always a bad thing?

Do you excel at making quick decisions or procrastinate?

In what ways do you think boys or girls have it easier?

What ways has jealousy made messes for you?

What makes you sad?

What age would you like to be for the rest of your life?

Whose mind would you most like to read?

Do you crave excitement?

What is a behavior you cannot abide?

If you could create something very beautiful, what would it be?

If you had an extra day every month that no one else had, what would you do with it?

Do you have a talent or special gift that you have not used?

What heroic attributes do you have?

What is a waste of time?

How many personalities do you have?

What is a more suitable first name for yourself (or another)?

What is your secret passion?

What one month on the calendar would you like to eliminate?

Do you prefer positions of leadership and authority?

How do you act when the pressure is on?

What is the one thing you would be willing to practice at least one hour a day until you became great at it?

What do you do when people do not admit that they are wrong?

Do you like or dislike challenges?

What are three things you think you need in order to be happy?

What rule is most important in your home?

What are some definite goals you are still working on?

Where is your largest time commitment?

What is a choice in life that you would never want to make again?

What are three barriers that keep you from reaching your full potential and what would help you overcome them?

How much do you use reward?

BY LAW, SHOULD . . .

*. . . HIV tests be mandatory for pregnant women
and people getting married?*

. . . smoking be banned in all public places?

. . . sex and violence on TV be eliminated?

. . . toy guns be banned?

. . . research that may lead to human cloning come to a halt?

*. . . children not graduate from high school
without being fluent in at least two other languages?*

What goes through your mind
when you see people on TV who
have endured great hardship?

What part of your life is "on hold"
now? What has to happen before
you can move on?

What are your embarrassments
and regrets?

Have you ever felt good about
doing something bad, inappropriate,
or illegal?

What do you want your funeral
to be like?

How private are you?

Do you encourage friends to drop
by your house without calling first?

What transitions in your life taught
you the most?

What have you learned from
your past?

Was there a moment that changed everything for you?

Do you put your interests first?

If you were imprisoned wrongly and then set free, would you seek revenge?

What is the best way to die?

If someone gave you a crystal ball, would you look in it?

What things, people, concepts, or ideas do you deeply hate?

Do you try to live by The Golden Rule?

Do you consider yourself pretty/handsome?

If there is a drug to enhance intelligence with no known negative side effects, would you take it?

If you could choose your height, how tall would you be?

If pills fulfilled nutrition and nourishment, would you take them and give up eating and cooking?

What do you think of the expansion of American fast-food restaurants and theme parks throughout the world?

Would you eat genetically modified food?

Would you participate in a study for a new medicine that could lengthen your life span?

Would you accept a heart transplant to save your life even if the heart donor were a pig?

Do you avoid eye contact?

What is something you have not yet done that you believe you can accomplish in your lifetime?

What are your life goals?

Do you feel that models in magazines give off the wrong signals by being so skinny?

What one thing would you like to change on your face?

How does one become a person of character?

How do you feel about the way you spend most days?

Are you good or bad at keeping secrets?

Do you prefer sunrise or sunset?

What would you like to build if you knew how?

What is your most attractive physical feature?

Do you like the way your voice sounds?

Have you been happy with the way you look?

If you got a tattoo, where and what it would be?

How do you feel about donating parts of your body at the time of your death?

Can nurses do doctors' work?

Would you submit to chemotherapy and under what circumstances?

What would you do if you found out you had AIDS?

Have you ever been addicted to anything?

How far should doctors go to prolong a person's life?

When do you exaggerate to make yourself look good?

What possession would you never agree to share?

What are you doing or did you do to escape a bad situation?

Do you analyze so much that you become immobilized?

Would you sign a request for a life-support machine to be switched off? When?

What signs of aging are you starting to see in yourself?

Would you have plastic surgery if finances were no object?

What is your best physical quality or feature and what is your worst?

Would you rather be healthy and homeless or have AIDS and live in luxury?

Does legalized gambling open the door for organized crime?

What item do you own has minimal dollar value but that you will not sell for any amount of money?

Do you think people of the opposite sex look better in long or short hair?

What do you think are the secrets to a longer, healthier life?

When telling stories or relating details of your day do you tend to exaggerate, understate, or be factual?

What five people would you take to a desert island and what would each contribute to the quality of life?

What aspects of other cultures would you like to incorporate in your life?

Would you rather try everything and not succeed or try only one thing and succeed?

What things would you not change about yourself?

What activity has most consistently given you a feeling of inner peace?

What things would you lie about?

What problem are you working on now?

When are you the most difficult to deal with?

What are your unfulfilled dreams?

Could you be incredibly rich and still have a good conscience?

If suddenly rich, what would be the biggest change to your lifestyle?

Do you consider yourself to be rich, upper income, middle income, lower income, or poor?

Is love of money the root of all evil?

If your accountant could set up a fictitious company for you in a tax haven and reduce the taxes you pay, would you go for it?

Are rich people happier than you, less happy, or about the same?

Should an embryo be transferable to anyone other than the biological parents?

WHAT WOULD YOU SAY OR DO IF . . .

. . . you were standing in line and someone cut in front of you?

. . . you were given a choice to either be a baby again or a fifty year old?

. . . you had $5 million to help other people?

. . . you knew that you were going to have a disabled baby early enough to terminate the pregnancy?

. . . if you had twenty acres of land and money to develop it as you choose?

. . . you got to choose how you are to die?

. . . you were chosen to join a space mission to colonize the universe and were that you would never set foot on Earth again?

. . . someone offered you $100 to shave your head?

At what age should birth control be allowed, especially the Pill?

Do you ever feel guilty about killing insects or rodents?

Can you be very poor but happy?

Is it okay to hunt for food?

Are medical experiments and testing of pharmaceutical products on animals justified?

Would you deliver a baby?

Would you rather be funny or kind?

What is the stupidest thing you have ever bought that seemed like a good idea at the time?

Would you rather be a famous national hero or discover a cure for a disease and be relatively unknown?

Would you shoot a burglar?

Is there anyone you now envy and why?

Would you rather give up your favorite food forever or television for two years?

Do you feel you have enough time/too much/not enough?

What are you most nosy about?

What is the most difficult thing for you to say "no" to?

Do you take others' behavior at face value?

Would you rather be known for your looks or your personality?

What would you do differently if you had no fear of making mistakes?

What lines do you not like to wait in?

Would you rather have X-ray vision or the ability to read minds?

Would you rather get $4 billion and be exiled from your homeland or stay and have little money?

Can a person ever be too rich?

Are you materialistic?

What is your greatest financial asset?

What "moment of glory" have you watched a friend have that you would like, too?

What is the most bizarre thing you have ever seen?

What smells make you nostalgic?

How strong is your sense of smell?

Are you more creative when alone or with others?

Would you rather be married to a famous person or be famous yourself?

Do you usually feel self-confident or not?

What are some little things that make you happy?

Are you good at "faking it" when you do not know what you are doing?

If you could choose something to dream about, what it would be?

Which things do you fear: failure, water, spiders, crowds, hair loss, injections, blood, sirens?

When was a time you felt guilty and how do you feel about it now?

How often would you be embarrassed if others knew exactly what was on your mind?

What not-so-heroic attitudes do you have?

Do you ever have cruel fantasies?

Which/who stresses you more: partner, family, boss, coworkers?

What is something you got rid of that you wish you had back?

What wakes you up in the middle of the night?

You get angry with yourself when you _____.

Which would be easiest for you to become addicted to: money, success, power, sex, alcohol, drugs, work, or TV?

Would you seek help if you had an addiction, or would you try to help yourself?

What in this morning's paper made you happy?

What is your greatest hunger besides food? Is it healthy or unhealthy?

Can you resist the temptation to inflate garden-variety disappointments or problems into catastrophes?

What is your most recent regret?

What was your last random act of kindness?

What was the smartest decision you have ever made?

What is something you said or did that still bothers you?

What seems to accumulate in great abundance in your life?

What is the focus of your life right now—relationships, goals, or objectives—and would you like to change that focus?

What would you like to be famous for?

What will be your next milestone in life?

Would you go to a nudist beach or camp?

Do you love animals?

Would you save your pet in a fire before you would save an enemy?

Would you buy an SUV or other gas-guzzling recreational vehicle?

What would it take for you to give up all your worldly possessions?

WHAT WAS THE WORST . . .

. . . storm you have ever been in?

. . . behavior you have ever witnessed?

. . . crime against humanity?

. . . thing that a sibling ever did to you?

. . . party you have ever attended?

. . . political crime you know of?

. . . travel experience you had?

. . . disappointment in your life?

. . . food you ever ate?

. . . book you have ever read?

. . . investment you have ever made?

. . . family trip you have ever been on?

. . . movie ever made?

. . . sexual experience in your life?

. . . New Year's Eve you have ever had?

. . . date you were ever on?

. . . holiday of your life?

. . . thing that ever happened to you in an elevator?

. . . home you have ever lived in?

. . . home decorating or fix-it experience?

. . . medical experience?

. . . place you have ever slept?

. . . experience you have ever had in a restaurant?

. . . car you have ever had?

. . . television series ever made?

Do you worry about dying?

What is the most shocking thing you could tell about yourself?

Are you mild- or hot-tempered?

What leading figure in a field would you like to hear speak?

What do you like least about your life?

Would you rather spend time or money on something?

What things can you do to feel less lonely?

What do you want to pass on to your children?

Are you good or bad at bluffing?

What is the worst rejection you have experienced and how did you handle it?

What is the most clever thing you have ever done for revenge?

When you see fresh flowers, do you usually take a few moments to breathe in their aroma?

What do you wish others knew or understood about you that you think they do not?

Do you keep your motives to yourself or do you share them?

When you look back on your life, what amazes you the most?

What was one of your most peaceful moments?

What was the most unforgettable coincidence you have ever experienced or heard about?

Are you regarded as a sensitive person or not?

Are you an emotional person?

Are you basically lucky?

Do you feel hurt if people do not try to cheer you up when you are unhappy?

What moment in your life would you like to replay?

What cares do you wish to drop?

Did you think that you would turn out the way that you have?

Do you prefer summer or winter?

Cigars: stinky or stylish?

What do you know so well and enjoy so much that you never accept less than the best?

Would you rather wake up early or sleep in late?

Have you ever tried to do the right thing and have it backfire?

Would you spend a week in an empty room?

When you make choices about right or wrong, do you consider mainly present or future consequences?

What was the most important decision you have ever had to make?

What was a kindness shown to
you today?

What are your disabilities?

With whom would you trade places?

In what ways has aging changed
your life?

Are you a retirement village type
of person?

What one thing most frightens you
about growing old?

At sixty-five, will you be broke,
still be working, be retired and
living comfortably, or be rich?

What would you like to "program"
your dreams to be?

What is a secret you keep from
almost everyone?

When you think of the next ten years,
what are you most excited about?

What are your greatest personal
concerns?

At what age does the quality of
life go down?

How would you like to spend the
last minutes of your life?

What do you look forward to the
most and the least about growing old?

How much money do you think you
will need for retirement?

To you, is aging decay or growth?

What do you do to restore your soul?

Have you ever witnessed something you just cannot forget?

What type of work would you like to do during your retirement for supplemental income?

Would you go peaceably to a retirement home?

When should people stop driving?

Do you feel children have a responsibility for the care of elderly parents?

How old do you want to be when you die?

At what age do you want to retire?

How would you make choices for a parent facing a long and agonizing physical deterioration?

How do you plan to have financial security for when you retire?

At 100 years old, what would you be doing and where would you be?

What does retirement mean to you?

Where do you want to retire and with what people?

Do you look forward to or dread retirement?

Could you retire in a college town?

Will you make a good old person?

What is your dream retirement?

At what age will you or did you begin
to slow down?

Do you prefer cremation or burial?

Describe yourself at eighty.

What do you take pride in?

Do you think Social Security will be
around when you retire?

Who are the oldest people you know?

How do you plan to spend the last
years of your life?

Would you clean the outside windows
of a skyscraper?

What is your interest in history?

Why do you think some people
are cruel?

Would you like to appear on TV?

What is one inhibition that would you
like to lose?

What new things would you like
to do?

What are life's compensations for
growing older?

Describe the perfect retirement home.

What elderly relative would you like
to get to know better?

What physical change do you worry
about most in the next twenty years?

Are you saving enough money for retirement?

What will be the sources of your retirement income?

Will you purchase your grave site while you are still alive or have it purchased for you when you die?

To what charity do you normally donate money or time?

Do you have a 401(k) account?

What kind of older person do you want to be?

When should health care be denied?

What personality traits would you like to cultivate?

What personality traits would you like to eliminate or manage better?

Would it disturb you if, after your death, your body were simply thrown into the woods to rot?

What is the best thing about growing older?

What provisions will you make for your parents if they cannot take care of themselves?

What natural phenomenon or act of nature would you like to see if you would be safe?

What would you hope to find if you traveled into outer space?

Do you think there is life elsewhere in the universe?

What are you thankful for?

Do you think genetically engineered foods are safe or dangerous?

Do you feel that global warming is a serious problem?

Do you think people will live under the ocean's surface 500 years from now?

What modern-day convenience do you consider a pain in the neck? What modern-day conveniences could you do without?

Do you obey rules you consider unfair or ridiculous?

Would you rather laugh or make others laugh?

In what situations would you like to be more bold and courageous or more assertive?

Would you rather avoid challenge or seek it out?

What are your feelings about the space program in general?

Where is the end of the universe?

Do you think the UFO information surrounding Roswell, New Mexico, is real or hype?

Are the rapid advances in technology helpful or harmful to you?

Should cloning be done at all?

DO YOU BELIEVE . . .

. . . in fate?

. . . in self-fulfilling prophesy?

. . . in "every man for himself"?

. . . in nature or nurture?

. . . you can truly escape your past?

. . . you can alter your mind-set without the help of drugs?

Would you clone yourself if you had the chance?

If you could "uninvent" one thing in the world so that it would no longer exist, what would you choose?

What new devices or machines would you like to have five to ten years from now to make life easier?

Do you think that life like that found on Earth exists in another galaxy?

What is something in nature you would like to bottle and sell?

Would you ever have your sperm or eggs frozen?

What would you do if you were diagnosed with Alzheimer's disease?

Would you rather wear a hairpiece or dentures?

How do the clothes you wear affect your moods and attitudes?

What is the one place you would like to lose weight the most?

What would you do if you went blind?

Are you self-conscious about
your height?

Have you ever felt so sick you wished
would you die?

Would you want to know if you
had cancer?

How often are you sick?

What are you like when you are sick?

What messages have you received
from others about your body?

What would you like a T-shirt to say?

You would jump up and down and
shout with joy right now if someone
told you _____.

What would you name your yacht?

How do you regard such things as
pierced noses etc.—offensive or just
bad taste?

What beauty tricks make you
look better?

If you were going bald, would you
shave your head?

Do you photograph well?

Would you rather go a week without
brushing your teeth or without taking
a shower?

Would you rather be sick at home for
a week or in the hospital for two days?

What would you do at an event where you are wearing the exact outfit that someone else is?

Have you ever been treated by a psychotherapist?

Do you feel you look better in long or short hair?

Do you think that the radiation emitted from cell phones is dangerous?

Do you tan or burn?

What kind or size of bed do you like?

Do you think older people look silly in tattoos?

When were you dressed inappropriately and felt out of place?

What was the greatest amount of physical pain you have ever endured?

What was your largest weight gain?

Would you rather be taller or shorter?

Is your way of tackling problems better than other people's?

With what tool, implement, or utensil do you feel most at ease?

Would you rather die by fire or by drowning?

Would being a hermit come easily or with difficulty for you?

If someone made a statue of you, what position would you choose?

Which interests you more: art
or politics?

Are you a gambler? Why or why not?

What would you like to own that
you do not already own?

Is less more?

What is one negative in your
life that you have been able to
turn into a positive?

What is the most difficult or
time-consuming task you have
done by hand?

Are you a predictable or
unpredictable person?

Are you a thinker or a doer?

Has anyone ever imitated
something you did or created?

Do you change your mind often
or stick to your guns?

Do you prefer day or night?

What is something you forgot once
that you will never forget again?

Where is it easiest for you to
have important talks?

Do you ever feel as if you do
not have anyone to talk to?

Who are three people you consider
to be geniuses?

When are you apt to cry?

What makes you feel guilty?

What do you like to do to lift
your spirits?

When have you acted phony?

Do you always want to have
the last word?

Politics

Do you question "conventional wisdom" and authority?

Of what ideas and lifestyles are you less or more tolerant of now than when you were younger?

How would you like to influence people's minds?

What is your first impression of a gay couple being affectionate in public?

Emphasis on efficiency: good or bad?

How do you know to trust someone?

Who is your favorite world leader?

Did you register to vote the second that you were eligible?

What institution do you have the most faith in?

Are we always responsible for what we do? What are the exceptions?

Which gender has the easiest lifestyle?

Sinking ship: women and children in lifeboats—what would you do?

What does it mean to act selfishly?

Does one particular issue drive your choice of candidates in federal and state elections?

What is one thing about living in this country that you value?

Would you ever run for political office? What would make you do so?

What is the institution you have the least faith in?

What is the silliest thing people do in general?

Which holds greater hope for the world: religion or science?

Do you feel that you are an ethical person?

What is your hope for the nation, for the world?

What is society's greatest barrier to peace?

What freedom do you value the most?

What is your first impression of a middle-aged Caucasian man driving a fancy sports car?

Is morality based on religious concepts?

DO YOU THINK . . .

. . . all people are created equal?

. . . most people are either born good or bad?

. . . it is a sin to "live in sin?"

. . . all, most, some, or no political candidates are pathological liars?

. . . the ends usually justify the means?

. . . that Congress does or does not cooperate with a president of the opposite party?

. . . selling off public lands to private companies for development is ever the right thing to do?

. . . government should regulate any industries?

HOW DO YOU EXPLAIN WHY . . .

*. . . a lot of bad people live long, happy lives
and innocent good people die?*

. . . we have laws and rules?

. . . radar detectors are sold if they are illegal?

. . . so many people have a drug problem?

Have you learned more from
successes or failures?

What is the thing that most limits
your freedom?

Do you consider suicide to be murder?
How do you think God views suicide?

What is the biggest change since
your childhood in the way people
act or think?

What is a fundamental truth
you hold?

What do you believe our individual
rights should be?

Are you sympathetic to the underdog?

What is your first impression of a
person in a military uniform?

What political, social, or moral cause
would you like to be more involved in?

Do you fight for your rights or give
up without much of a struggle?

Who would you like others to
think you are?

If you got conflicting news reports, which source would you be most inclined to believe: radio, TV, magazines, or newspapers?

What is the most important piece of information you have picked up in life so far?

Do you concentrate on one great cause?

Has anything that happened to you changed all your priorities?

What would you like to see on the cover of major news magazine in the near future?

What is the human situation?

Do you "buy American?" Is buying American important to you?

What do you think about rich people who pay little or no income tax?

What is your favorite provision of the Constitution?

Does the IRS abuse its powers?

Do you think lower-income people pay their fair share, too much, or too little income tax? How about middle-income, upper-income, and you?

What do you think is good about the world?

Would you ever be frozen if promised you could come back?

Is allowing unapproved experimental drugs to be marketed worth the risk of exposing patients to undiscovered side effects?

Would there be more advantages or problems if nobody ever died? What would they be?

If you had fifteen minutes of prime-time TV, how would you use it and what message would you share?

Who is solving the big problems in the world?

What problem, if solved, would give you the greatest peace of mind?

What are restrictions that you cannot stand living with?

What is one item that symbolizes the times in which we live and why do you see it as a symbol?

Can you explain logical positivism or moral relativism?

What does a conscience do and where does it come from?

Can people and nations be grouped and stereotyped?

Are you typical of your generation?

Technology: time saver or not?

What are five people, places, or things that define the American style?

Share a hope and a fear you have about the future.

What needs to happen to truly experience freedom?

Where are you likely to find untold treasures?

What areas of research do you feel should be broadened?

What is one thing in life that you care most deeply about?

Are certain nationalities, races, religions, political parties, or countries better, smarter, more industrious, etc.?

If you had to, could you kill someone in war?

Is there any cause you would be willing to die for?

What truth have you learned that you want to share?

What are your definitions of injustice and victimization?

Who are the five top brains?

What unethical things have you done?

Do people generally have common courtesy and manners?

People are most influenced by _____.

Could you stand up for something you thought was right, even though many may disagree?

If you were alive in the 1960s, would you have been a hippie?

WHAT WOULD YOU DO IF . . .

. . . a close friend or family member
who is terminally ill asks you to help him or her die?

. . . you had absolute power over other people?

. . . you got the freedom you always wanted?

. . . you were a smoker in a nonsmoking place?

. . . you were invisible for a day?
Is there some wrong you would right?

. . . you witnessed a drug deal?

Which would you like more:
fame or success?

What is the perfect age and why?

What famous person's life
story do you think every adult
should know about?

What have you contributed to the
welfare of the planet?

What does "cool" mean to you?

What is your favorite country?

What is your first impression
of a suspect being restrained by
a police officer?

What advantages do the youth of
today have that you did not have?

How do you know "right"
from "wrong?"

Would family and friends describe
you as ethical?

When is surrendering a weakness
and when is it a strength?

What are things you have not
made your mind up about?

What is your favorite piece of
common sense?

If your life philosophy could be
summarized on a T-shirt, what
would it say?

Is there a weaker sex? Which one?

What was the most important
idea of this century, last century,
and of all-time?

Time machine: where would you
head first?

Who is the most independent,
original thinker you know?

What is your first impression of an
African American male driving a fancy
sports car?

Should Columbus Day be a
national holiday?

If you could have a different
point of view, how would you like
to see the world?

What would be the advantages and
disadvantages of one language for the
whole world?

Home HIV tests: a good or bad idea?

Does state-sponsored gambling
really create jobs and stimulate
local economy?

What do you think about using tax money to support private schools?

Where should funding of the arts come from?

What gives you the best value for your tax dollar: military defense, police, public broadcasting, public schools, or _____?

What should be the energy resources of the future?

What is your first impression of an underage pregnant woman?

Who was the most important role model in your life?

What behavior of yours that does not represent the real you do you want to change?

What is your first impression of a rock video with scantily clad women?

What are three questions you would like a world survey of?

If you could experience another culture firsthand, which one would it be and what intrigues you about it?

What are three things you feel totally neutral about?

What is a reason for which you would seriously contemplate suicide?

What will you not tolerate no matter what?

What human behavior do you find the most discouraging?

What thought or sentiment would you like to put in fortune cookies?

What wall, boundary, or border would you like to dismantle somewhere in the world?

Do you have confidence in big business?

Have you ever gone against popular political opinions or beliefs?

What are some of the most tragic things happening in our world?

Should gay couples have the right to marry?

Do you think capital punishment acts as a deterrent?

What should be the use of American military forces beyond our borders to apprehend alleged violators of U.S. law?

Should the identity of jurors be protected in criminal trials?

What do you think about the anti-land mine campaign?

WOULD YOU RATHER . . .

. . . be rich and alone or poor with lots of friends?

. . . have no rules or live with the ones that exist?

. . . go to war or be a conscientious objector?

. . . drive a tank during a war or work on an aircraft carrier?

. . . be a liberal or a fundamentalist?

How should Medicaid and Medicare work, and what are possible improvements?

What are your feelings about pornography?

Should there be secret/classified government documents?

What was the biggest news event during your life so far?

Can nuclear war be prevented?

Have you ever marched for or against anything?

How do you feel about guns?

Are you more accepting of racial diversity than your parents?

How should military expenditures be regulated?

While growing up, what did war mean to you?

What do you think about allowing people to view executions?

What should the minimum punishment be for those who commit white collar crimes?

What two people would you like to see in the next presidential race?

Do you favor or oppose a law forbidding the sale of all alcohol?

What heavy luxury tax should be imposed?

Is there more or less crime in your city
or area than a year ago?

Do you have confidence in
organized labor?

What should prisoners contribute
to society while locked up, besides
license plates?

What should be changed about
the American electoral system?

How would you fix "the system?"

Is there a case in which stealing
is legitimate?

Atrocity photos: do they manipulate
the public?

Are all politicians a little crooked?

What do you think should be
done about election campaign
financing limits?

Do you support life imprisonment
without parole for major drug dealers?

What is interesting to you in the news?

If sex with minors was legal, would
you do it?

What do you think of the creation
and use of an international language?

Should you be able to sue
the President?

Should there be a law requiring
a husband to be notified if his wife
decides to have an abortion?

Should government educate people about the environment?

What are your thoughts about prison and forgiveness?

What do you think of the "three strikes" laws?

What do you do with recyclables?

How do you support the use of renewable energy?

Is our President honest and trustworthy?

What do you think the Republican Party's relationship with women is?

Should neighbors be warned about sex offenders?

What should be the punishment for child abuse?

Should health insurance cover infertility treatments?

What do you think about condom distribution in high schools?

Are you optimistic or pessimistic about the nation's future?

Do you have confidence in TV news?

What revision of current parole laws would you make?

What is the most important election issue for the federal government?

What was the most interesting legal case of the past year?

Do you think the judicial system is fair, too lenient, or too tough in sentencing criminals?

What three questions should every American have to answer?

Do we really need the CIA?

Should animals be used in medical and scientific experiments?

What measures should be taken to save endangered species?

Do you consider yourself as being PC or fear not being PC enough?

Does the NRA reflect your views about guns?

Have you ever taken part in the Gallup or Roper Poll or other public opinion surveys?

To reduce crime, will it help to have more police?

Should taxpayers support professional sports teams with new stadiums and tax breaks?

Genetic engineering: beneficial or unnatural and potentially harmful?

What are your thoughts on the role of the UN?

What are government policies' effect on moral values?

What do you think about feeding the poor and malnourished in the United States and elsewhere?

WHAT IS YOUR OPINION . . .

. . . of the draft?

. . . of the death penalty?

. . . of equal rights for homosexuals?

. . . on increasing surveillance of U.S. citizens by the government?

. . . on gun control and gun licenses?

. . . of drug control efforts?

. . . about giving the U.S. military the power to aid police in antiterrorist activities?

. . . of the U.S. military?

. . . of the possible legalization of drugs?

. . . of monopolies?

What event in American history do you most vividly remember?

What do you think about sexual harassment in the military and in military academies?

Should doctors inform patients about the alternatives to abortion?

Which local social service agencies are effective?

What is the most regrettable event in U.S. history?

Who should be overseeing the safety of prescription drugs?

What is media's impact on our knowledge of world events?

What existing law would you eliminate?

If asked to serve in a war that you felt was unjust, what would you do?

What is the price of peace?

What does "peace on earth" mean to you?

What great accomplishments or world developments have occurred during your lifetime?

How old is too old to be President?

Should English be our official language?

What do you know about the RU-486 abortion pill?

What prominent politicians have you met?

What do you think about enforcing payment of criminal fines?

Would you turn in a lawbreaker or play it safe?

What news stories bother you?

Do you fear nuclear war?

Do you have a favorable or unfavorable opinion of Hillary Rodham Clinton?

What are your thoughts about Osama bin Laden and the efforts to find him?

What are your thoughts on the Social Security system?

What is the first step toward resolving poverty?

Do you vote by party or by
the person running?

Do you have confidence in the
Church or organized religion?

What do you think about allowing
women on combat aircraft or ships?

Should the national anthem
be played before sporting and
other entertainment events?

Should prayer in school be prohibited?

What should be the fate of draft
resisters or dodgers?

What else might nations do, besides
war, to settle their differences?

Should science classes in schools teach
an alternative to evolution?

What do you think about deactivating
air bags?

What would a world peace-keeping
system be like?

What should be done about
the problem of drug abuse in the
United States?

Is American society basically racist or
are incidents isolated?

What do you think the length of a
presidential term and the number of
consecutive terms should be?

What is your perception of
immigrants to the United States?

What should be done about
the intrusive coverage by modern
journalism?

Are any illegal acts justified under
certain circumstances?

Would you cut off federal
welfare benefits to people who
have not found a job or become
self-sufficient in two years?

What are the ways you believe the
government lies to us?

What was America's lowest national
moment in your lifetime?

Have you ever been the target
of prejudice?

Do you support the United States'
building a defense system against
nuclear missiles?

Do you think we should try
reestablishing U.S. diplomatic
relations with Cuba?

Who do you think should be
added to Mount Rushmore?

What do you think about
Medicare and Medicaid?

Should libraries get free books
from publishers?

Have you ever boycotted companies
that sponsor conservative causes?

What do you think of the repatriation
of Native American burials?

What do you think the punishment should be for senior management officials when they commit stock fraud and similar crimes ?

How do you feel when a TV program is interrupted by a special news bulletin?

Do you have confidence in the police?

What evidence of racist attitudes have you witnessed?

How important is it to you to vote in local and national elections?

What are our nation's moral values?

What do you think about limiting the number of terms for Congress and the Senate?

Who was the best President in your lifetime, the President you admired most in your lifetime, and also before your lifetime?

What do you think NATO's and the UN's involvement in the internal affairs of countries should be?

Do you think that electioneering for President should start at a designated time before the election?

Have you ever run for any office?

What presidential candidates did you think were a joke?

What do you think of the issue of assisted suicide?

What do you think the federal funding of public TV and radio should be?

Can you be nonviolent in a conflict
with a violent adversary and survive?

Do you believe in the death penalty
or do you think it should be banned?

Should doctors be allowed to end the
life of a patient who is about to die
and is or will experience great suffering
(i.e., doctor-assisted suicide in life-
threatening situations)?

What section of the newspaper do you
most like to read?

What should be done about criminals
acquitted on technicalities?

What can be done to stop child
slave labor?

What would be your priorities
list for Congress?

Which Vice President would have been
a great President?

Should the death penalty be legal?

Do people generally have respect
for the law?

What is the first step toward
resolving racism?

Do you favor or oppose a
constitutional amendment to permit
prayer in public schools?

What do you think about the rate of
violent crime in the United States?

The human organ shortage: should we
pay for donated organs?

HAVE YOU EVER...

... seen firsthand the damage war can do to people or places?
... had the urge to kill someone?
... thought of joining the Peace Corps?
... thought of running for a political office?
... been an anarchist?
... switched political parties?
... marched in a protest or rally?

What new law would you like to make?

Is reverse discrimination a real problem?

What should be done about unsolicited junk mail, e-mail spam, and phone solicitation?

What should be the priority: exploring space, the ocean, or our planet?

How should racial epithets be treated?

Which concerns you more: the nation's economic or moral problems? Are they related?

If there was no need for armies, how should government use the money?

Would you tell the FBI about a family member you knew committed or was suspected of committing a crime?

What do you think about the availability of health care coverage in the United States?

Should there be a limit of legal immigrants to the United States?

Should more stringent measures be taken to prevent illegal immigrants from entering the country?

How should the identification and deportation of illegal aliens be handled?

Do you believe in doctor-assisted suicide in nonimmediately life-threatening cases?

What should be the penalty for illegally dumping or disposing of nuclear waste?

Do you see abortion as a major presidential issue?

What big wartime event affected you?

Do you have confidence in the criminal justice system?

Are "three strikes" laws the answer to violent crimes?

Who should be sponsoring the arts?

Do you have confidence in the medical system?

Which fertility practice do you think needs regulation?

What do you think about the controversial development around a national monument or battlefield like Gettysburg?

What can you do personally to eradicate racism?

Do you define yourself politically as liberal, moderate, or conservative?

How do you react to littering?

What was your verdict in the O. J. Simpson trial?

What do you think should go on the site of the former World Trade Center?

What can be done about overcrowding in prisons?

Do you engage in political protest?

Have you ever given testimony in court?

Do you have confidence in newspapers?

Do public officials really care what people think?

What is your confidence in the police force?

Do you worry about terrorist attacks?

Known disabilities: would you abort or give birth?

Would you report a rape or sexual assault?

How much do you think people should get for something like silicon breast implants that they chose but that ended up being dangerous to their health?

Do you support the death penalty for persons convicted of murder?

How should we be dealing with
the terrorism issue?

Do you think the location of
battered women's shelters should
be unpublished?

Should it be illegal to manufacture,
sell, or possess semiautomatic guns
(assault rifles)?

What should the fine be for
running a red light?

Should marital rape be a crime and
punishable how?

How do you think the problems in the
Middle East could be resolved?

Should victims have more rights
and criminals less?

The Middle East: are your
sympathies more with the Israelis
or the Palestinians?

What steps have you taken to
conserve water?

What is our country's most pressing
problem today?

What would be the effect of
women on national security if they
were used in direct combat?

What is your overall opinion of Iran?

What did you think of the
Whitewater scandal?

What did you think about the
Monica Lewinsky scandal?

What do you think about stopping all legal immigration into the United States for the next five years?

Whose politics have you admired?

Do you believe every person is racist?

How do you think the world would be different if all the world's leaders were women?

When do you make up your mind for voting: in the voting booth, days before, the week before, or long before the election?

What steps have you taken to prevent the depletion of the ozone layer, global warming, and the greenhouse effect?

What should be done to regulate government expenditures and eliminate waste in the U.S. government?

Do you own a flag and display it?

How would you rate the current President?

Would you perjure yourself to protect someone you love?

How harmful do you think secondhand smoke is?

Do you think that smoking should be banned from bars everywhere?

What would the world be like without superpower nations?

What patriotic gestures have you made?

Should there be a law requiring private companies to retrain employees who lose their jobs to mergers and downsizing?

What do you think the campaign issues will be in the next presidential election?

Is it too easy to get a divorce?

Do you think we should establish a new system where federal campaigns are funded only by the government?

What do you think about the global village concept?

What do you think about abortion when a woman or a family cannot afford to raise the child?

Should government promote any particular set of values?

RIGHT OR WRONG?

Ebonics?

Prostitution?

Downloading music files without paying?

Abortion in first three months, second three months, and final three months?

Marijuana?

Gay marriages?

Drafting of women?

Charter schools?

DO YOU . . .

*. . . favor or oppose the RU-486
abortion pill as a prescription drug?*

*. . . interact on a personal level with
people outside your racial or ethnic group?*

. . . follow the results of public opinion polls?

*. . . have an understanding of how
public opinion polls are conducted?*

. . . think the FBI has a file on you?

*. . . think race relations have improved or gotten
worse in your lifetime?*

. . . eat only "dolphin safe" tuna?

Why do you think it is that you cannot vote until you are eighteen, but you can drive a car from the age of sixteen?

What issue do you feel strongly about but have kept to yourself?

Microsoft: Bad Big Brother or Good Guy?

What government position do you think you would be great at?

What will be the most powerful nation in 100 years?

What is your overall opinion of Mexico?

What do you think about the speed or lack of speed of FDA drug approval?

Is society biased against single women?

What should be the punishment for
Nazi-era deeds?

What rules should exist
concerning smoking?

What should the antidrug
methodology be: law enforcement
or education?

If you were on a jury, could you
send someone to death if he or she
was found guilty of murder?

Immigrants: are they a serious threat
to Americans' jobs?

Why do you vote for "your"
political party?

Is the federal government
doing a good or bad job of
governing the country?

What do you think the size and role of
the federal government should be?

Does the President have a clear plan
for solving the country's problems?

Should Microsoft be made to
be less of a monopoly?

What would you say to the President
if you had fifteen minutes alone?

Should all parolees or probationers
pay for their own supervision?

Which President do you think had
the greatest impact?

If you were the only one to witness a
crime, would you report it?

In what ways are men discriminated against: paternity leave, retirement age, legal voice over abortions, more rights in divorce settlements, and child custody?

Should we have laws to prohibit state and local governments from giving preferences in jobs or school admission on the basis of race?

What is a government policy you strongly disagree with?

What should be done with hazardous waste and what are alternatives for its removal?

How widespread is racism in American society?

What is one function in our culture that you would like to see become more efficient?

Can a husband who abuses his wife be trusted with his children?

Should it be illegal to perform abortion in the last six months of pregnancy except to save life of the mother?

Do you favor or oppose teaching about gay/lesbian orientation/lifestyles in public schools?

Do you think you would make a good politician?

Does media have a liberal bias or a right-wing bias?

What steps have you taken to prevent
the destruction of the rain forest?

Should the government do more or
less to solve our country's problems?

What should be the punishment
for incest?

Do you support foreign aid in the
form of military assistance?

How were you affected by the terrorist
attacks of September 11, 2001?

Have you mostly voted for winners
or losers?

How would you solve littering
problems?

Are you a Republican, Democrat,
or Independent?

How can we begin to transform
our culture?

If your election were guaranteed,
would you run for public office? If so,
which? If not, why not?

Is government run by a few big
interests or mostly for the benefit
of all people?

If you were the President of the
United States and could change one
thing, what would it be?

Do elected officials care more
about being reelected than doing
what is right?

Do you believe America is respected?

What do you do about issues that bother you?

Who should be overseeing the soundness of financial institutions?

What revision of the welfare system would you make?

Should women murderers face the same kinds of punishment as men?

What should America's role in world affairs be?

Are all tests inherently culturally biased?

What should be done to drunk drivers who kill?

What should the minimum punishment be for those who rape?

Televised trials: do cameras belong in the courtroom?

Do you keep up with current events?

What causes have you fought for over the years?

Would you report a possible case of child abuse?

What can be done for refugees seeking asylum?

How can we get rid of gangs and gang violence?

In what ways might your own attitudes be racist or bigoted?

Do you think state governments should be authorized to handle welfare?

Have you personally been a victim of racism?

Does the President share your values?

What role should the United States play in the New World Order?

If you could be assured that the President would really read and answer your letter, what would you write?

What one politician would you like to see out of office?

SHOULD WE BE SOFTER OR STRICTER ON . . .

. . . juveniles who commit crimes?

. . . people who commit racial injustices?

. . . those who download music for free from the Internet?

. . . those who commit fraud and corruption in the medical, legal, and insurance fields?

. . . people who physically abuse their spouses?

. . . pedophiles?

. . . underage drinkers?

. . . gamblers?

. . . drunk drivers?

. . . people who jump turnstiles in subways?

. . . people who do not buckle their seat belts?

. . . graffiti artists?

What is your overall opinion of Israel?

Is the convenience of human
beings more important than the
protection of nature?

What are the effects of bad news
in the media?

Define our responsibilities in
a democracy.

Would you advocate government
force when necessary?

Do you support genetically
modified foods?

Have you ever boycotted
produce because of growers'
unfair labor practices?

When do you think cellular phones
are bothersome or obnoxious?

Should there be a law requiring a
twenty-four-hour waiting period
before an abortion procedure is done?

How has your view of politics
changed since you started voting?

Did you ever falsify a time card,
report card, or expense report?

Should alcoholic beverages be
sold online or via mail order?

What is the most regrettable event
in international history?

What was the most compelling
news story of the past year?

If a person "supports his or her own kind," is he or she being racist?

What campaign slogans do you remember?

Who should be overseeing the safety of food products?

What kind of leader are you most apt to follow?

What news events have fascinated you?

What issue concerns you the most and what have you done about it?

Could a woman be an effective President of the United States?

When do you think the first nonwhite person will be sworn in as President?

If you were head of the country, what rules would you make so citizens would be well educated?

Should there be an equal opportunity to die in combat, on police duty, or by capital punishment?

How do you feel about the nuclear arms race?

Do you think the United States should be aiding the poor in other nations?

Should hunting animals be legal?

Why cannot a nuclear weapons freeze be negotiated?

How do TV political ads influence your decisions?

Are politicians more or less capable nowadays than they used to be?

What do you do to protect your privacy?

Do you favor reduction in size and budget of all government agencies?

Do you refuse to cross picket lines?

How fearful are you of terrorism?

What should be done to clean up land mines?

What was the best debate you have ever watched?

What do you think about abortion when pregnancy was caused by rape or incest?

How can society prevent the spread of sexually transmitted diseases?

What event raised your understanding of the larger world?

What direction do you think the country is going in?

How do you stand on the issue of abortion? Are you pro-life or pro-choice?

Do you have confidence in the presidency?

Should a woman's life be spared before a man's?

You would fight in a war if _____.

Does the federal government
do a good or bad job on commercial
air safety?

What should be done to enforce
payment of child support?

What do you think about equality
in the military?

What do you think should be
changed in the immigration
regulations for the United States?

Should sex offenders be chemically
castrated?

What do you think about
homosexuals in the military?

Should there be a law requiring
women under eighteen to get
parental consent for abortion?

If the leaders of our nation followed
the views of the public more closely,
do you think the nation would be
better or worse off?

What should happen to people who
inflame religious and ethnic hatred?

Do you think that homosexuals
should or should not have equal
rights in terms of marriage and
job opportunities?

What do you think about
prohibiting all noncitizens (even
legal residents) from contributing
to political campaigns?

How young is too young to
be President?

WHAT WOULD YOU DO IF . . .

. . . the President tried to end a strike and failed?

. . . the draft was reinstated?

. . . your best friend wore a fur coat to your party?

. . . terrorists started to attack U.S. cities on a frequent basis?

. . . your significant other became extremely politically active?

. . . carcinogenic chemicals were discovered in your backyard?

What do you think a world government might be like?

What are the most hopeful signs of progress in race relations?

How can problems with border patrols be dealt with?

What would be your strategy to fight the war on drugs?

How would you battle an unscrupulous manufacturer?

What are your thoughts about the right and responsibility to vote?

What do you think about government-funded school vouchers for the school of the parents' choice (public, private, or parochial)?

Do you have confidence in the military?

What environmental issue concerns you the most?

What should be the percentage of federal spending for social programs such as health, education, and welfare?

Does the United States interfere too much internationally?

Should newspapers print quotes from unnamed sources?

Would you break the law in certain situations? Which ones?

What should be the legal rights of gays and lesbians in regard to marriage and benefits?

Should people have the right to defend themselves, their family, and property by all available means?

What is outlawed that you wish was not?

What should the penalties be for breaking environmental laws?

Should the President intervene in labor disputes?

Is enough done to prevent terrorism in the United States?

What do you think about large cuts in funding for welfare?

FDA drug approval: is the system working?

Does our President get things done?

Would you still vote for your last presidential choice if the election was held now?

Intellectual property agreements:
are they fair?

What would be a good alternative to
prisons? What do you think about the
problem of prison overcrowding?

Do you check to see if something is
printed on recycled paper?

Would you report software piracy?

What precautions for shipments of
hazardous materials should be taken?

What was America's grandest national
moment in your lifetime?

Would you classify tobacco as
a drug and regulate it?

Do newscasters portray news
with accuracy?

What do you think about limiting
the amount of money labor unions,
businesses, and industries can
contribute to House and Senate
campaigns?

Would you vote for or against a
constitutional amendment to require
a balanced federal budget?

Are fertility doctors going too far?

Would you say there is more or
less crime in the United States than
a year ago?

What do you think about
reducing federal spending for
military and defense purposes?

What should be the pollution
and emission controls?

Would you vote only for a candidate
who shares your views on abortion?

Should cigarette companies be
held legally responsible by families
of smokers who died of smoking-
related causes?

What should be done about the cost
of health care in the United States?

What should the punishment be
for apartheid-era crimes?

Which political party is more
interested in education?

Should a child's life be spared
before an adult's?

Are there too many or not enough
sexual harassment lawsuits?

What were the saddest stories
of the past year?

What do you think about
international intelligence gathering?

WHAT IS YOUR OPINION OF . . .

. . . the welfare system?

. . . the fight against organized crime?

. . . the fight against drugs?

. . . the fight against cancer?

. . . a strong police force?

. . . more funding to the military?

What would be a great new site for the U.S. President's home?

What other Presidents besides Richard Nixon do you think were corrupt?

What do you think about limiting the amount of money individual citizens can contribute to political parties?

Do you think that the welfare system should exist and what should be its place in the future?

Do people really have a say in what government does?

What should the regulations be for pornography on the Internet?

What act of injustice troubles you?

Should the sentence be fixed for certain offenses or should it be based on evidence and circumstances?

What contributes most to tension between the races?

Should every citizen be entitled to free Internet?

What do you think about having national health insurance and socialized medicine?

How do you feel about people with extreme political views?

Who was the most attractive politician in history?

Do you think abortion should be legal under any circumstances, legal only under certain circumstances, or illegal under all circumstances?

What progress do you think our nation has made with the drug problem?

How do you feel about news media's coverage of the presidential campaign?

What interactions have you had with the police?

Do you think the warning on cigarette packages means anything to smokers?

Do you know your local politicians personally?

Are you often or never unsure of whom to vote for?

Have you ever worked on a political campaign?

Is there a particular law you have pretty much always disregarded?

What do you think of requiring people to vote, not just giving them the right?

What friends, neighbors, and relatives of yours were involved in a war?

Have you ever witnessed a serious crime?

Do you have confidence in the public schools?

Would you be a good political campaigner?

Do you follow local government doings?

Would a king have been better than a president for the United States?

Do you think presidential term limits should be abolished?

Do you buy only "cruelty-free" products?

What do you think the Democratic Party's relationship with women is?

Do we need a third political party?

What do you think the postal system of the future will be like?

What should churches' involvement in political matters be?

Spirituality

What is sacred?

How does God speak to you?

Who made the world and
who made God?

Could you ever be a religious leader?

The Bible: fiction or nonfiction?

What biblical event would you like
to have witnessed?

Do you have a special memory of
Sunday school or confirmation?

Are you familiar with the beliefs
of other spiritual traditions? Is there
one that particularly interests you?

Do you read or have you read
the Bible?

What additional commandment
would you add to the ten?

If somebody or something does not fit
your system of beliefs, what do you do?

What was your most spiritual
moment?

Have you ever had psychic intuition
or premonition?

Do you know about the teachings
of the Buddha? What do you think
of the Dalai Lama?

Have any predictions for you
come true?

What prayer did you feel was
answered and what one was not?

Would or did you have a religious wedding ceremony?

If you believe in life after death, where do you think you are going or what do you think you are coming back as?

Do you read astrology column(s) regularly?

What is heaven like?

Would you marry someone with different religious beliefs?

Would you marry someone who is atheist or agnostic?

If you could ask God one question, what would it would be?

When did you first read the Bible?

Would you ever elope? Would that suit you? Would it hurt your family and/or friends?

What have you learned from reading the Bible?

How has your spirituality changed since you were a child?

What crisis pushed you closer to God?

Do you believe in good luck charms?

Do you worry about whether you will go to heaven?

What is a new belief system(s) you adopted and how did it change your life?

DO YOU BELIEVE . . .

. . . that a house can be haunted?

. . . people can hear from or communicate with the dead?

. . . televangelists are legitimate?

. . . in the Ten Commandments?

. . . that there is a God who cares?

. . . in miracles?

What is your expectancy of going to heaven?

Should the church stay out of politics?

Why do you think televangelists are so popular?

What should be the role of prayer in childhood?

What beliefs would you go out on a limb for?

What things do you pray for presently?

What one of the Ten Commandments is most important to you?

Are you superstitious about a black cat crossing your path, walking under a ladder, the number 13 or 666, breaking a mirror, or knocking on wood?

Have you changed a deeply held belief because of practical experience?

What animal would you like to be reincarnated as?

How do you pray?

Does the Bible have a happy ending?

What teachings of your church confused you?

Do you think that God sees everything?

What does the Sabbath mean to you?

Does God love some people more than others?

Does prayer help save people?

Have you ever doubted there was a God?

Was there a time when God did not seem to exist?

Do you believe in superstitions and how superstitious are you?

With what belief have you struggled?

Who is the most spiritual/religious person you have ever met?

Have you ever had predictive dreams?

What person most influenced your spiritual life?

Have you ever had any out-of-body or déjà vu experiences?

If you are presently attending church, how did you come to join it?

Do you believe humans have souls?

What is the first thing that comes to mind when you think about God?

WHAT IS YOUR FAVORITE . . .

. . . Bible passage?

. . . biblical character?

. . . prayer?

. . . church or temple?

. . . spiritual pick-me-up when feeling blue?

What were the three superstitions you heard most while growing up?

What was the funniest thing that happened in a religious setting?

What spiritual leader would you like to learn more about?

What parts of the Bible do you like best or which had meaning for you?

Do you believe in the afterlife and reincarnation?

What do you wish your parents had told you about their spirituality?

Who do you know is psychic?

Can you learn to use intuition?

Tell about something your spirituality motivated you to do.

Where do you do pray and where do you worship?

Have you ever witnessed a seemingly supernatural event?

Have you ever changed your religion?

Why were we created?

What have you given up for
your religion?

Do you believe in voodoo?

Do you think that most wars were
started because of religious conflict?

Talk about forgiveness.

What does baptism mean to you?

What cults and religions give
you the creeps?

Is organized religion for you, or are
your beliefs more alternative?

Was religion important during your
teen years?

Do you believe in heaven's existence?

Would you ever donate money to
a televangelist?

Do Ouija boards or crystal balls
really work?

Do you believe in déjà vu?

Do you ever feel you were here in a
previous life?

When was there a time when
incredible faith was required of you?

How important was religion to your
family when you were young?

What do you really believe in?

Is it important for a Christian to
attend church?

Do you believe animals have souls?

Do you believe in angels?

Do you think religion is increasing its influence or losing it?

Is taking communion meaningful for you?

Which of the Ten Commandments is most ignored today?

What benefits do you see in believing in a higher power?

Do you usually believe people who tell you that they have seen an angel or had a similar religious experience or do you think that they are basically crazy?

Were you ever active in a religious youth organization? Why or why not?

If you are presently attending church, what would you like to change about it?

Do have you an active spiritual life?

Do you explore your spirituality alone or with others?

Will God answer your prayers?

Are there things people should not pray for?

In what situation would it be awkward for you to talk about your spirituality?

What do you look for in a church?

Who have you prayed for most and why?

What person from the Old Testament do you admire?

Should the Bible be a sourcebook for instruction?

Where would you build your temple or place to practice your spirituality?

Have you had any personal experiences with God?

Are you becoming more spiritual as you age?

Have you ever had a religious epiphany?

Who prays for you?

When was a time you felt forgiven?

What is your involvement with religion as an adult?

What are your most important spiritual goals?

WHAT DO YOU THINK . . .

. . . about claims to having a vision of God or Jesus?
. . . about going to church versus praying on your own?
. . . God's gender and/or race is?
. . . of atheists and agnostics?
. . . of Catholic clergy celibacy?
. . . of the possibility of new religions?
. . . of women as priests, rabbis, clerics, etc.?

Has God ever spoken to you and what did He or She say?

What does God look like?

What parent most influenced your spiritual development?

What three questions would you like to ask God?

How do you feel right now about religion?

Did you resent or enjoy church and/or Sunday school?

Who is a friend who really lives his or her spirituality?

Do you believe in ESP, telepathy, telekinesis, clairvoyance, or channeling?

Do you believe that it is possible to divine the future?

Where is the presence of God in a sometimes hostile world?

When between Thanksgiving and Christmas does your holiday spirit peak?

Do you believe there are witches?

What are the most influential experiences of your life?

Do you believe in God?

What pastor/priest/etc. did you feel closest to and why?

What cults would you have belonged to?

How did the example of your parents' spirituality influence your desire to pursue that same spirituality?

Do you ever try to convert others to your religion?

What effect has nature had on your spirituality?

Have you had a close brush with death or other spiritual experience that changed your life?

What are your first memories of attending a religious service?

Have you ever known any born-again Christians and how did you feel about them?

What book or article had an impact on your spirituality?

Do you believe in the Devil or demons?

Do you believe people can be possessed by the Devil or demons?

Is your intellectual life compatible with your spirituality?

Do you pray? Why and how often?

Do you believe there is a hell? If so, how can you keep from going there?

What religions have you explored and rejected?

Did/do you and your family attend religious services?

Would you ever boycott a product, service, movie, book, or play for a religious reason?

What were the most important religious holidays in your childhood home?

How important would you say religion is in your life?

What was your religious training growing up?

What is a concern you have about your spiritual life?

Have you had any telepathic or paranormal experiences?

What are your church memories from childhood?

Do you believe all religions are basically the same?

What was the role of prayer in your childhood home?

How many of the Ten Commandments can you list?

What are the qualities you love about being human?

Where do you perceive abundance and/or lack of it in your life?

Do you believe in karma?

What do you consider as a necessary evil(s)?

What ways have you changed for the better because of your spirituality?

What is it about spirituality that brings us so much satisfaction?

What experience fills you with peace?

Have you ever practiced visualization?

Do you believe we are descendants
of Adam and Eve?

Has anyone ever made fun of you for
what you believe?

What important decisions have
you based on intuition?

Would you live your life differently
if you knew that you were going to
die soon?

Why do you think bad things
happen to good people?

What is your individual purpose
on Earth?

What religious place would you
like to visit?

Does your happiness outweigh
regret in general?

Do people have heroes or heroines
any more?

How do you feel about your life
right now?

Have you ever experienced the
feeling that you do not really exist?

What is your metaphor(s) for life:
life is like _____.

Do you believe in destiny or choice?

Do you believe America is truly
tolerant of all religions?

DESCRIBE . . .

. . . a supernatural event, real or imagined.
. . . an experience you consider close to a miracle.
. . . a higher plane of existence.
. . . God.
. . . an alternative to a god.
. . . what your religion will be like in 100 years.

Do you expect miracles?

How would your life be if you only listened to your inner voice?

What is your biggest regret?

Do you want others to act the way you do?

How would you prefer not to die?

What places do you go to in your mind when you want some peace and quiet?

Would you like to live forever?

Have you ever felt detached from your body and everything else?

Have you ever tried meditation?

Does yoga help bring your mind to another plane?

Why do you think we look out from an individual body and point of view?

What about beauty draws us to it and why does it makes us feel good?

What hunches have you had lately
and how did you use them?

Do you feel that you give off
more positive or negative karma
in your daily life?

What is the greatest leap of faith
you have taken?

Does free will exist?

Do you think God designates
how long each person will live or
He or She allows circumstances
to determine that?

What are your reasons for wanting
to go on living?

What is your idea of paradise, either
before or after death?

How long do you think you will live?

How long would you like to live?

What are the things you used to be
afraid of?

In what areas do you have some
"healthy disbelief"?

If you were a plant, you would be
_____.

What would you like to say to adults
who wish they were children again?

What is one superhuman ability you
would choose to have?

What could you take less seriously?

Are there unforgivable acts? What are
they and why?

Do you believe in the power of self-transformation?

What are three steps you need to take to become the person you were meant to be?

What things can you prove are true?

Is there any religion you are not be interested in exploring?

Have you ever consulted: horoscopes, a palm reader, tarot cards, runes, Chinese astrology, a psychic, tea leaves, or I Ching?

What prayers, chants, and sayings make you feel better?

Are you yin or yang?

Do you think the world is becoming more spiritual or less spiritual?

Work

Do you believe people are basically lazy or hardworking and why?

How will you earn your fifteen minutes of fame?

What talent would you like to have more than anything?

What are the "teachers" and "classrooms" in life and what should we do to earn an "A" in life?

If 100 people your age were chosen at random, how many do you think would be leading a life more satisfying than yours?

What is the most boring thing you can imagine doing?

Do you believe that playing is more important than winning?

Do differences in social standing reflect what people have made of their opportunities?

Have you ever felt like a fraud or impostor and that others might find out you are not so great and that you have reached your level of competence?

Are you pursuing your big goals every day?

Define "the good life."

What is the longest project you have ever worked on?

How do you measure a person's success in life?

Is failure always bad and success always good?

What is the right choice between a man and a woman equally qualified for a managerial position when there are no other women at the top?

What do you think about the availability of good jobs in the United States?

What was your first "real" job?

Would you transfer to a different state than you live in now for a job?

What would your occupation have been in the Old/Wild West?

In what ways do you make your boss look good?

What was the profession you often mentioned when people asked what you were going to be when you grew up?

What occupations do you find despicable?

In what ways do you wish you could change your business history?

What could you do to become the best at your profession?

What is the most likely reason someone would want to join or leave your company?

What do you have in and on your office desk?

If you were the boss, what changes would you make at work?

WOULD YOU RATHER . . .

*. . . fail in business and be bankrupt or fail
in marriage and be divorced?*

. . . deliver babies or pizzas?

. . . take care of animals or people?

. . . work for the FBI or NASA?

. . . be a dentist or a dress designer?

. . . be a cartoonist or a sports columnist?

. . . work hard to gain what you want or have it given to you?

. . . be a police officer or a firefighter?

. . . be a librarian or a chemist?

. . . work outdoors with your hands or indoors at a desk job?

*. . . receive daily encouragement from your boss
or a 5 percent raise?*

. . . work for a pleasant boss or for yourself?

. . . work at a job that was challenging or one that was easy?

. . . be a farmer or a politician?

*. . . have a high-paying job and travel 50 percent of the time
or an average-paying job with no travel?*

. . . be highly educated or highly successful?

. . . play more or accomplish more?

Is it easy or hard for you to find jobs?

Would you prefer to work at
a desk that you primarily sat down
at or stood up at?

How many hours do you work
each week?

In what ways have you seen racism
at work?

Did you have to work during college?

What would your dream office be like?

What company, organization, or institution would you like to run?

What is an occupation you think would be fascinating?

What is one job you would like to have back?

Will big-business mergers hurt consumers?

Would you change careers?

What is the best way anyone could compliment you about your work?

What are the most- and least-rewarding parts of your job?

What would it take for you to leave your job?

How many times have you changed careers or line of work?

Have you changed your occupation?

What five projects do you wish you were presently involved with?

How important are unions in protecting the rights of workers?

What would be your company's epitaph if it went under tomorrow?

What is most important to you concerning a job?

Are minority quotas necessary in hiring?

If you won the lottery, what would
you choose to do for a living?

Have you ever taken a sick day
when not sick?

Is your organization a Ferrari,
a Ford Taurus, or a VW Beetle?

What work assignment(s) have you
particularly hated?

What inventions make your job easier?

What job on a movie crew would you
like to have?

What responsibility or work did you
dislike while growing up but that
proved very helpful to you as an adult?

What different careers would
you like to have if you had to make
a change every seven years?

What was the most difficult
paycheck you have ever earned?

Do you love your work?

Are you satisfied with your
current salary?

Have you ever lied to keep your job?

What is something satisfying
about your work?

Where is the most interesting
destination you have ever had to
travel to for business?

What was the dirtiest job you
have ever had?

How hard do you think you work?

What professions require the skills you have and love?

What work-life issues plague teenagers with jobs?

How many jobs have you had?

Do you think smart kids should skip college to start their own companies?

Would you accept a less enjoyable job for twice what you make?

What has been your motivation to achieve or succeed in your career?

How important is putting in "face time" at work?

Do you display your pet's picture at work?

What are some false or outdated assumptions people operate under at work?

What was your first self-supporting job?

How can you become more knowledgeable and current in your field?

Would you respect a boss less if he or she smoked cigarettes?

What do you think about the wife as the primary wage earner?

What do you think about the President stepping into a labor dispute?

What new position would you like to attain at work?

How would you deal with the emotional turmoil of losing a job?

As a teenager, what were your part-time jobs?

Have you ever worked as a waiter or waitress?

How can you get paid for doing what you love?

What is an unusual occupation of a friend or relative?

Have you worked mostly with men or women?

Which gender do you prefer as bosses?

Which gender do you prefer as subordinates?

What early jobs did you have?

Do you like to be told what to do or be your own boss?

If you made a huge mistake at work, would you admit it or pretend it had nothing to do with you?

What was the most unusual job you have ever had?

On a typical work day, what takes up most of your time?

Have you ever cried at work?

How stressful is your job?

Why should you be hired over other candidates for a job?

How do you advertise yourself?

Are you hard-working or lazy?

What occupation will have the highest salary in fifty years?

What job would you like to have for one month?

Do you have an ultimate career goal?

What would have been your dream career?

What is your idea of the Utopian workplace?

What ideas do you think would help your company improve quality, save money, and increase sales and productivity?

When was a time you lost a job?

How often do you lie at work?

Who would you trade jobs with and why?

Have you ever worked unusual hours?

How do incompetent and obnoxious people manage to keep their jobs?

Of what accomplishments in your career are you the proudest?

What have been the high points of your career(s)?

How much did your first job influence your later career?

What is something you would like
to shout at your boss or coworkers?

What is the next challenging
assignment you would like to have
at work?

What type of work would you like
to be doing five years from now?

Which do you prefer to do business
with: a small company or a giant?

You have striven to be what kind of
worker with what qualities?

Do you agree with your employer's
policies and procedures? Have you
gone against any of them?

What professions or occupations
are actually more harmful than good?

How did your level of education
influence your career?

Have you ever been a victim of
harassment on the job?

What good business tips have
people given you?

What businessperson do you
particularly admire?

Does your work keep you awake
at night? Why?

What is the simple secret of success
in the work world?

What project(s) have you worked on
that did not turn out as planned?

Tell a story about a favorite boss.

What promotions have you had?

Have you ever been passed over
for a promotion and what did you
do about it?

What occupational certifications
would you like to achieve?

What kind of company culture and
environment are ideal for you?

What additional career education
would you like to attain?

What higher educational degrees
would you like to achieve?

What business or company do
you wish you owned?

Would you like to have your
significant other working for you?

Do you have a calling?

What is the most innovative practice,
service, or product your organization
has launched in the past year?

Where did you get started in
your career?

What changes would you like to
see made at your company?

What odd jobs have you done?

Have you ever dated anybody you
met at work?

Would you take a golden
parachute plan?

IF YOU COULD . . .

. . . hire a personal assistant, what would he or she do for you?

. . . have had any job in history, what would it be and why?

. . . work fewer hours in exchange for less pay, would you?

*. . . choose what hours and days you work,
how would you schedule your forty hours?*

*. . . trade work skills the way kids swap baseball cards,
who would you trade with and for what skills?*

. . . start your own business, what would it be?

*. . . create a new, unique position for yourself in your
organization, what it would be?*

What unnecessary work interruptions and trivial matters could you do without?

What are the most popular lies people tell at work?

How would you react to having to listen to New Age music at work for motivation?

How might technology affect your job in fifty years?

Have you ever run your own business? How did you start it?

Do you wish you worked more or fewer hours a week?

Who is the most naturally gifted person you have ever worked with?

Which interests and economic factors led you to certain career choices?

How do you think your mate feels about his or her career?

Have you ever worked at a fast-food restaurant?

Do you enjoy physical work or mental work?

Have you ever taken supplies from work?

Do you prefer to work alone or with a group?

What work assignment(s) have you particularly enjoyed?

Would you be working in a different profession if it paid more?

Do you often have several projects going at once?

How did where you earned your degree influence your career?

In what way has affirmative action affected you?

Have you ever been discriminated against at work?

What is something important on your desk?

Are you working too hard?

What would you want to be if talentwise it was possible?

What are your present major projects and ventures?

At work, do you make most of the decisions?

What job could your company not pay you enough to do?

What would be a practical alternative to business cards?

What should be the minimum number of paid vacation days dictated by the government?

If a female employee is told by a male supervisor that she looks good, is that sexual harassment?

Do you think women have the same opportunities as men to get jobs or be promoted?

Which high position in your government, industry, religion, or education would you want?

If you were a mail carrier, what weather would bother you most?

Have any major setbacks occurred in your career(s)?

Who has helped you up the ladder?

Are you happier working backstage or as the leading actor?

What people outside your family have been laid off or fired in the past year or the last economic downturn?

What is your most important work-style quality?

What is the current state of your career?

What about work most reminds you of what you disliked about school?

Would you report a too-large paycheck?

What do you do at your home desk?

How far would you go to get a job you desperately needed?

Should employers be able to cite diversity as the reason for using race to determine who will be laid off from a job?

Have you ever had a secretary?

If you had the option to never work again, would you take it?

What do people at your job grumble about most?

In what field of endeavor would you like a two-hour crash course?

Do you enjoy what you do at work?

Would you ever work for your significant other as a subordinate?

What methods would solve the unemployment issue?

Do you know how to properly format a letter?

What do you do when asked to work overtime?

What companies and/or institutions have you worked for?

What is your main opinion of job sharing and other parent-oriented benefits?

What should companies provide for
child care benefits?

What would your ideal job
or career be?

How much is your personal identity
and self-worth determined by your job
and your success at it?

What would you like to be when
you grow up?

What was the most unpleasant job
you have ever had to do?

Do you work on weekends,
on vacation?

Have you ever worked at a resort
or in a resort area?

Are you a glutton for overwork?

If you were financially independent,
would you continue to work?

Are you a better talker or listener?

Talk about responsibility.

How much time per day do you
devote to yourself?

Are you practical or ingenious?

How forgetful are you?

Would you put off having kids
for a career?

Have you ever given advice
when you really did not know
what you were talking about?

How do you handle compliments?

Are you nimble with your hands?

Where do you want to be in five years?

Have you ever been fired or laid off?

If you did not have to worry about making a living, what would you most like to do the rest of your life?

What are three things you would most like to accomplish in the next year?

Were you ever given real help and encouragement in finding out what you wanted to do?

Do you ever daydream about future events? How often?

What are the best and worst business decisions you have ever made and how did they affect your life?

Career or custody of child: should women have to choose?

How do you feel about your schedule?

When did you begin using a computer and why?

Which forms of affirmative action make sense in fields that have typically excluded women in the past?

Would you leave your job if your significant other got relocated?

What obligations should you eliminate or say "no" to?

Do you think it is better or worse when management and rank-and-file mix?

What is your feeling about changing jobs?

Would you want the security of staying at the same company all your life?

Are you a relentless worker?

Have you been paid fairly at jobs throughout your life?

Who would you fire: poor performer/great person or good performer/disliked person?

Should recruitment of women be encouraged in engineering, law enforcement, construction, etc.?

Would you feel more loyalty to a union or your employer?

If you had a choice, would you work at home or commute?

What management fads have driven you crazy?

Is it easy or hard to adapt your behavior to the company you are in?

Is the government adequately regulating business mergers?

Has fear of sexual harassment lawsuits affected your office?

What would motivate you to work seven days a week, twelve hours a day for a month on an important project?

Have you ever wanted your boss's job?

Are you scared of people in authority?

What business ideas are in your thoughts presently?

What contracts have you signed?

What makes you nervous at work?

What do you think about the portable workplace?

Who was the most difficult boss you have ever had to deal with?

Do you believe a person is defined by what he or she does for a living? Why?

Have you ever invented an item on your résumé?

What intangible benefit makes your work worthwhile?

Do you take initiative or just do what you are told?

What would you do if a lie detector test was required for a job?

What honor would you like to attain at work?

Do you confuse yourself with your job?

What is the harshest job advice you have ever received?

What should be businesses' commitment to their workers and communities?

Are you instinctively good at business matters?

Do you stay later at work than intended?

DO YOU . . .

. . . agree or disagree that it is important to have a good hard failure when you are young?

. . . take more or fewer sick days from work than most people?

. . . take shortcuts to get your work done fast?

. . . define yourself by your job or other things?

. . . socialize with coworkers?

. . . feel confused if you are interrupted while working?

. . . call yourself ambitious?

. . . worry that you will lose a job?

Does creating a harassment-free workplace invade staffers' privacy?

What things do you like about your work?

What interests do you share with your coworkers?

Do you meet or miss deadlines?

What do you think about the difficulty of applying for a grant?

Do women still need affirmative action?

Have you ever lied to get a job?

What motivates you most to go to work each day?

What would your company be like if you had never worked there?

What job would you most or least like to have during the holiday season?

Would you leave your job to pursue
a singing career?

If you were alive 150 years ago,
what job would you have had?

What is the best word to describe your
current work situation?

What kinds of jobs did you have
as a kid?

What do you enjoy doing, even
consider fun, that most others
regard as hard work?

Do you prefer a career or a job?

How much energy have you spent
in finding your calling?

Do you think people would be
surprised about your thoughts?

Does your work define your identity,
or is it defined by family role and
personal interests?

Have you ever had a mentor?

Have you ever been a mentor?

What would make your life easier?

When discussing your career with
others, do you tend to exaggerate,
understate, or be factual?

What was the most creative or exciting
place you have ever worked?

What company had the best
lunchroom at a workplace?

What invention would make your job
much easier and more productive?

What were the most challenging working conditions you have ever had?

Have you ever made personal phone calls from work?

Do you consider your work an escape from the pressures of home?

What is your leadership style?

What was your first job and how did it influence your career? What did you get paid?

What coworkers have you particularly liked or were memorable?

When you look at someone who is hugely successful, do you think of him or her as a lucky person who was in the right place at the right time?

Do employees without kids work harder?

Are you jealous of people who have experienced more career success than you?

Do you have any advice on choosing a career?

Were you encouraged to explore all your talents and interests no matter how often they changed?

Do you get excited when talking about your work?

Do you eat lunch at your desk?

Describe your best-paying job.

What is the most important work
skill to have?

If you came up with a brilliant idea,
who or what might prevent you from
implementing it?

What work wraps you up and
carries you away?

Can you predict exactly what you will
wear to work every day this week?

If you were to be fired or promoted,
what would be the most likely reasons?

What do you think about drug
screening of employees?

What is your best excuse for not
going to work?

What occupation do you think will be
popular in fifty years?

Are you too amenable or too good-
natured at work?

At your workplace, what type
of excuse for leaving early would be
most acceptable?

Have you ever gone on strike
or have to deal with a strike at
your workplace?

What about you led to your
career choices?

What are the most important
things you can do in your job within
the next twelve months?

What things would you rather be
doing when you are at work?

WHAT IS YOUR FAVORITE...

...place for a business lunch?

...thing to put on after work?

...day of the workweek?

...thing to do after work?

...word-processing software?

Would you prefer to be a research scientist or a senator?

What should all companies provide for all employees?

Where would you like to relocate your workplace?

Should employees have a say in the salaries of their superiors?

What is needed to make "work" more fun?

What things do you do to make it through a tough workday?

Are you willing to pay the price of success?

What is your greatest creative ability or gift?

Do you use your talents at work?

Do you like to take or give orders?

What was the first time you discovered power?

What is your major concern about big-business mergers?

What is your job stress level?

Do you have any desire to be the President of the United States?

Do you think success at work is more likely if you improve the way you look?

How often do you feel others are better, smarter, richer, happier, or more successful than you?

Have you ever achieved a success without experiencing fulfillment?

What is your favorite way of wasting time?

What do you consider wasting time to be?

What is the highest honor you have ever received?

ABOUT THE AUTHOR

Dr. Barbara Ann Kipfer is a lexicographer and archaeologist. She is the author of more than twenty-five books, including the best-selling *14,000 Things to Be Happy About* and *Page-a-Day* calendars based on it. She has also authored *Instant Karma, The Wish List, 1,400 Things for Kids to be Happy About*, and *8,789 Words of Wisdom*. Her other books are *Roget's 21st Century Thesaurus, The Order of Things, Roget's International Thesaurus*, 6th ed., and *The Flip Dictionary*. She has an M.Phil. and Ph.D. in linguistics, a Ph.D. in archaeology, and an M.A. in Buddhist studies. Dr. Kipfer is the senior lexicographer of Lexico, the parent company of Dictionary.com, Reference.com, and Thesaurus.com.